High Speed Rail

Presented to Parliament
by the Secretary of State for Transport
by Command of Her Majesty
March 2010

Cm 7827

£26.60

Photographic acknowledgements

Front cover: Southeastern
Alamy Images: pp23, ALSTOM Transport: pp131, Alvey and Towers: pp7, 137
National Railway Museum/SSPL: pp119, Rail Images: pp11, 58, 81, 96, 142, 149,
UIC: pp37

The Department for Transport has actively considered the needs of blind and partially sighted people in accessing this document. The text will be made available in full on the Department's website in accordance with the W3C's Web Content Accessibility Guidelines. The text may be freely downloaded and translated by individuals or organisations for conversion into other accessible formats. If you have other needs in this regard please contact the Department.

Department for Transport
Great Minster House
76 Marsham Street
London SW1P 4DR
Telephone 0300 330 3000
Website www.dft.gov.uk

© Crown Copyright 2010

The text in this document (excluding the Royal Arms and other departmental or agency logos) may be reproduced free of charge in any format or medium providing it is reproduced accurately and not used in a misleading context. The material must be acknowledged as Crown copyright and the title of the document specified.

Where we have identified any third party copyright material you will need to obtain permission from the copyright holders concerned.

For any other use of this material please contact the Office of Public Sector Information, Information Policy Team, Kew, Richmond, Surrey TW9 4DU or e-mail: licensing@opsi.x.gsi.gov.uk.

OS maps are reproduced from Ordnance Survey material with the permission of Ordnance Survey on behalf of the Controller of Her Majesty's Stationery Office © Crown copyright. Unauthorised reproduction infringes Crown copyright and may lead to prosecution or civil proceedings. Department for Transport.

ISBN: 9780101782722

Printed in the UK by The Stationery Office Limited
on behalf of the Controller of Her Majesty's Stationery Office

ID 2352648   03/10

Printed on paper containing 75% recycled fibre content minimum.

Contents

Foreword   5

A National Strategy for High Speed Rail   7

Executive Summary   11

Part 1: The Case for High Speed Rail

1. The Twenty-First Century Transport Challenge   24
2. Capacity, Connectivity, Sustainability   42
3. Supporting Growth in the Regions   55
4. A Core High Speed Rail Network   64

Part 2: High Speed Two – London to Birmingham

5. London to Birmingham   80
6. High Speed Two – The Route   97
7. High Speed Two – International Connections   120
8. Design Standards and Regulation   127

Part 3: The Way Forward

9. Engagement and Consultation   134
10. Planning Consents and Construction   138
11. Costs and Funding   141
12. New Industry, New Jobs   144

Conclusion   151

Foreword

Britain's future prosperity depends upon investing in technologies that drive economic growth. High speed rail has a crucial role to play.

New national networks will be essential. In telecommunications, the Next Generation Fund will underpin the provision of fibreoptic broadband throughout Britain. In energy, the need to enhance supply whilst reducing carbon emissions is requiring huge changes in how we generate and distribute electricity. Our transport networks will also need to be radically enhanced.

Britain pioneered the railways in the nineteenth Century, and in the thirty years from 1959 it built a national motorway network. More recently, short haul aviation has developed a sizeable market. Taken together, these networks will not be sufficient – or on their own suitable – to fulfil Britain's inter-city transport requirements for the twenty-first Century. New inter-city networks will be required to enhance both capacity and the connectivity of our major urban economies. But they need to be sustainable, and consistent with the imperative to reduce carbon emissions.

Across the world, high speed rail is helping to achieve these objectives. Not only France's TGV and the pioneering Japanese Shinkansen but new high speed networks across Europe and Asia are increasing capacity, slashing travel times, transforming the connections between cities, and offering the most comfortable and convenient travelling experience in history. Where high speed rail connects cities in less than about three and a half hours, traffic moves en masse from the plane to the train. It is striking that countries which have built a first high speed rail line have gone on to build more.

Even the US, where passenger railways fell into virtual disuse in the post-war decades, is now looking to make a decisive leap to high speed rail, in place of yet more domestic aviation.

Britain's High Speed One line, from St Pancras to the Channel Tunnel, shows what can be achieved. Completed on time and on budget in November 2007, High Speed One has cut journey times from London to Paris and Brussels to around two hours and seen rail's share of the travel market to these cities grow to over 70 per cent. The introduction of Javelin high speed domestic services last December has radically reduced journey times to London from towns across Kent, opening up major growth and regeneration opportunities.

Over the past year, HS2 Ltd – a Government appointed company – has developed detailed, costed and deliverable options for a high speed line from London to the West Midlands, and assessed a range of possibilities for a wider network which could stretch to the North and to Scotland.

This Command Paper sets out the Government's proposed strategy for High Speed Rail. As a first stage it proposes the development of a core high speed rail network linking London to Manchester and Leeds via Birmingham, with high speed services connecting directly to other cities in Northern England and Scotland from the outset.

Over the coming months the Government will consult widely on these proposals, with a view to legislating to take forward a project in the light of the responses.

High speed rail has a transformational role to play at the heart of Britain's twenty-first century transport infrastructure. This Command Paper sets out a plan for the future. The next step is for a national debate to begin.

Gordon Brown
Prime Minister

Andrew Adonis
Secretary of State for Transport

A National Strategy for High Speed Rail

In January 2009, the Government established High Speed Two Ltd (HS2 Ltd) to consider the options for a new high speed rail network in Britain, starting with a costed and deliverable proposal for a new line from London to Birmingham.

HS2 Ltd's report was presented to the Government at the end of December 2009. It is published alongside this Command Paper today. It concludes that there is a strong business case for a new London to Birmingham line, and sets out detailed recommendations for the design of its route, together with a range of options for how it might be extended to serve other conurbations.

The Government has evaluated these proposals in respect of their costs and benefits for enhancing capacity and connectivity in a sustainable way, which is its key strategic objective for inter-city transport. As part of its analysis, it has also considered other realistic options for meeting the UK's inter-urban capacity needs over the next 30 years, including carrying out a detailed analysis of the potential costs and benefits of major improvements to existing rail and road networks.

On the basis of this evidence, the Government's assessment is:

1. That over the next 20 to 30 years the UK will require a step-change in transport capacity between its largest and most productive conurbations, both facilitating and responding to long-term economic growth;

2. That alongside such additional capacity, there are real benefits for the economy and for passengers from improving journey times and hence the connectivity of the UK;

3. That new capacity and improved connectivity must be delivered sustainably: without unacceptable environmental impacts, and in line with the Government's strategy to promote a low carbon economy, including its statutory targets for reducing emissions of greenhouse gases;

4. That high speed rail is the most effective way to achieve these goals, offering a balance of capacity, connectivity and sustainability benefits unmatched by any other option;

5. That high speed rail should form an essential part of a wider strategy for sustainably enhancing national, regional and local transport networks in the UK that includes policies for managed motorways, rail electrification, and the increasing uptake of low carbon vehicles;

6. That Britain's initial core high speed network should link London to Birmingham, Manchester, the East Midlands, Sheffield and Leeds, and be capable of carrying trains at up to 250 miles per hour. This Y-shaped network of around 335 miles (see indicative map on page 14) would bring the West Midlands within about half an hour of London, and deliver journey times of around 75 minutes from Leeds, Sheffield and Manchester to the capital. HS2 Ltd's work has shown that as a first step a high speed line from London to Birmingham would offer high value for money as the foundation for such a network, delivering more than £2 of benefits for every £1 spent;

7. That the initial core 'Y' high speed network should include connections onto existing tracks, including the West and East Coast Main Lines, so that direct high speed train services can be operated from the outset to other cities including Glasgow, Edinburgh, Newcastle and Liverpool. Consideration should be given to extending the network subsequently to these and other major destinations to further improve capacity and connectivity;

8. That the capacity released through transferring long-distance services to this network should be used to expand commuter, regional and freight services on existing lines, with particular benefit for areas expected to see significant housing growth including Milton Keynes, Luton, Northampton, Peterborough, Kettering, Corby and Wellingborough;

9. That HS2 Ltd's recommended route for a London-Birmingham high speed line ('High Speed Two'), which would run from a rebuilt Euston station in London to a new Birmingham City Centre station at Curzon/Fazeley Street, is viable, subject to further work on reducing specific impacts on the local environment and communities;

10. That following completion of that further work, formal public consultation on the Government's proposals for high speed rail in the light of HS2 Ltd's recommended route for such a line should begin in the autumn;

11. That HS2 Ltd should now begin similar detailed planning work on the routes from Birmingham to Manchester and to Leeds, to be completed in summer 2011, with a view to consulting the public early in 2012;

12. That effective integration with London's current and planned transport networks is crucial, and that this is best delivered through the combination of a Euston terminus and a Crossrail Interchange station sited between Paddington and Heathrow, which would also provide a link to the Great Western Main Line;

13. That a second interchange station located to the south east of Birmingham would be of value in enhancing access to the high speed line for the West Midlands, and offer direct links to Birmingham Airport, the National Exhibition Centre and the M6 and M42. Such a station should be included in the core project, subject to an acceptable funding package being identified;

14. That high speed rail access to Heathrow is important, and should be provided from the outset through a fast and direct link of about 10 minutes via the Heathrow Express from the Crossrail Interchange station;

15. That, as foreshadowed in paragraph 57 of the Government's 2009 Decision on Adding Capacity at Heathrow, further assessment is needed of the case for a potential station at Heathrow Airport itself. The Government has appointed Lord Mawhinney to assess the options, and their respective business cases, taking account of the work published today by HS2 Ltd, the study already underway by the airport operator, and the proposals that have been put forward for a station at Iver;

16. That the new British high speed rail network should be connected to the wider European high speed rail network via High Speed One and the Channel Tunnel, subject to cost and value for money. This could be achieved through either or both of a dedicated rapid transport system linking Euston and St Pancras and a direct rail link to High Speed One. HS2 Ltd will carry out further work to assess the viability and cost of each of these, including a full assessment of the business case, prior to any public consultation;

17. That powers to deliver this proposed high speed rail network should be secured by means of a single Hybrid Bill, to be introduced subject to public consultation, environmental impact assessment and further detailed work on funding and costs to feed into decisions to be taken in the next Spending Review. Depending on Parliamentary timescales and approval, this could allow construction to begin after the completion of London's Crossrail line, opening from 2017, with the high speed network opening in phases from 2026;

18. That HS2 Ltd's estimated £30 billion cost for a core high speed rail network linking London to Birmingham, Manchester and Leeds reflects its finding that construction costs for major projects in the UK are higher than for comparable projects elsewhere in Europe. In the light of this evidence, Infrastructure UK

will work with the Department for Transport to consider whether and how civil engineering costs can be reduced, and further work on HS2 Ltd's cost estimates may be required following the completion of that work;

19. That the funding options for high speed rail should be further developed by the Government, taking particular account of the scope for securing third party contributions towards the cost of constructing new lines and stations;

20. That a long-term programme of investment in high speed rail would present significant new opportunities for the UK's design, engineering, construction and manufacturing sectors; enable the development of skills and expertise in the UK's rail industry supply chains; and promote UK firms' expertise and competitiveness in the global high speed rail market;

21. That a strategy of this kind can only be developed and made a reality through active and open engagement with those who will be affected by or who are interested in it; and that, well before formal consultation starts in the autumn, HS2 Ltd should engage with local authorities and representative groups, including those representing key minorities, to ensure that the consultation can be as effective as possible.

This Command Paper sets out both the Government's response to HS2 Ltd's recommendations and its assessment of the case for an initial core British high speed rail network, on the basis of the evidence presented by HS2 Ltd and its own analysis. It will be the subject of formal public consultation and further review and assessment before any final decisions can be taken on either the strategic case for high speed rail or the specific routes that any line may follow.

The Government proposes to begin formal public consultation in the autumn, to cover three key issues:

- HS2 Ltd's detailed recommendations for a high speed line from London to the West Midlands
- The strategic case for high speed rail in the UK
- The Government's proposed strategy for an initial core high speed rail network

Part 3 of this document sets out in more detail the Government's plans for public engagement and consultation.

Executive Summary

The Twenty-First Century Transport Challenge (Chapter 1)

Demand for travel between the UK's largest cities is expected to increase significantly over the coming decades, driven by continuing economic growth and rising prosperity. This has the potential to see congestion and crowding gradually worsen across all modes of transport, leading over time to slower, less reliable and more uncomfortable journeys for travellers, and potentially endangering the long-term health of the UK economy.

The Government is taking action to address these challenges and, in line with Sir Rod Eddington's recommendations[1], is focusing substantial investment on improving the capacity and performance of existing networks.

For rail, some £25 billion will be invested in capacity enhancements in England and Wales over the next seven years, including at least 1,300 extra railway carriages, major line and station upgrades in Reading and Birmingham, and the Thameslink

---

1   The Eddington Transport Study (2006) http://www.dft.gov.uk/about/strategy/transportstrategy/eddingtonstudy/

and Crossrail schemes to transform capacity and major north-south and east-west commuter routes into London. The recently completed modernisation of the West Coast Main Line has substantially increased rail capacity to Birmingham and beyond. Electrification and additional rolling stock are also planned for the Great Western Main Line and on commuter routes in the North West.

On the strategic road network, motorway widening and the innovative use of hard shoulder running at peak times on the M42 near Birmingham, together with improved real time information for motorists, offer the prospect of sizeable capacity and reliability benefits. The £6 billion roads programme announced in January 2009 is rolling out this approach much more widely, alongside a number of targeted motorway and strategic road widening schemes across England.

But there is a limit to the improvements that can be squeezed out of our current transport system. The same railway lines that provide inter-urban routes north of London must also support the capital's commuter market, as well as regional and freight services. As a result, they are already close to carrying as many services as they can.

Further major upgrades to the existing network would be highly expensive, problematic and disruptive. The West Coast Route Modernisation project cost £8.9 billion and took almost a decade. It delivered fewer benefits than originally envisaged and caused serious disruption to travellers and to business, at a significant economic and social price in addition to the cost of the project itself.

Given the extended timescales for planning, developing and delivering major schemes, it is therefore vital that work begins now to identify how best to ensure that the UK's transport infrastructure can continue to support and facilitate a successful twenty-first century economy.

Improving capacity and connectivity cannot be the sole objectives for new national transport infrastructure. It must also be sustainable.

Transport projects bring substantial social and economic benefits, but they can also impose costs through their impacts on individuals, communities and the environment, including through the carbon emissions that they generate. In developing the UK's future transport networks, therefore, the Government's objective is to bring forward transport projects which will deliver the greatest improvements in capacity, connectivity and performance whilst minimising these negative impacts.

The Strategic Case for High Speed Rail (Chapters 2 and 3)

The Government has considered a wide range of options for addressing Britain's long-term inter-city transport challenges, taking into account their impacts on capacity, connectivity and sustainability, as well as their financial costs. These included new motorways and railway lines, both conventional and high speed, an expansion in domestic aviation, and a number of major packages of improvements to existing networks.

In respect of improving the networks linking England's principal conurbations, the Government has ruled out major new motorways and an expansion of domestic aviation on sustainability grounds. The growth in car travel enabled by entirely new major motorways would increase greenhouse gas emissions substantially, over and above the local environmental implications of such schemes. And new motorways would not in any case provide significant time savings for city centre to city centre journeys. A major expansion in domestic inter-city aviation is considered by the Government – in line with the Committee on Climate Change's advice in December 2009 – not to be a viable option due to long term constraints on aviation capacity.

A detailed analysis has been carried out by the Government of the potential costs and benefits of improving existing road and rail networks, alongside the work done by HS2 Ltd on the case for new high speed and conventional railway lines.

This assessment indicates that major, multi-billion pound upgrades to existing road and rail networks would provide far less additional capacity than a new railway line. Major upgrades also involve considerable disruption for travellers. Moreover, they yield few of the connectivity improvements which new high speed routes make possible – for example, transforming links between the West Midlands and other conurbations in the Midlands, the North and Scotland, in addition to substantially improving journey times to London.

While entirely new conventional rail lines could address the long-term capacity constraints on the rail network, their net costs would be almost as high as those of high speed rail without delivering anything close to the same journey time benefits.

High speed rail, in contrast, delivers against every one of the Government's key objectives. It offers dramatic connectivity benefits and journey time savings between major urban centres. It provides very significant capacity increases for long-distance travellers as well as releasing space on conventional networks for increased commuter and freight services. And it achieves this whilst remaining consistent with the Government's overall strategies for reducing greenhouse gas emissions.

Furthermore, HS2 Ltd's work suggests that a well-designed and managed high speed rail project, despite its substantial costs, could deliver high value for money, with well over £2 of benefits for every £1 spent.

On the basis of this analysis, the Government's assessment is that high speed rail should be at the heart of its long term strategy to transform the UK's inter-urban transport networks.

A core high speed rail network for the UK (Chapter 4)

In comparison to other European nations, Britain's economic geography is tightly packed, with relatively short distances between its major cities, especially in the Midlands and the North. Journey times and capacity between the UK's four largest conurbations – London, Birmingham, Manchester and Leeds – could be transformed by a Y-shaped high speed rail network of around just 335 miles of high speed track, capable of carrying trains at up to 250 miles per hour.

High Speed Rail

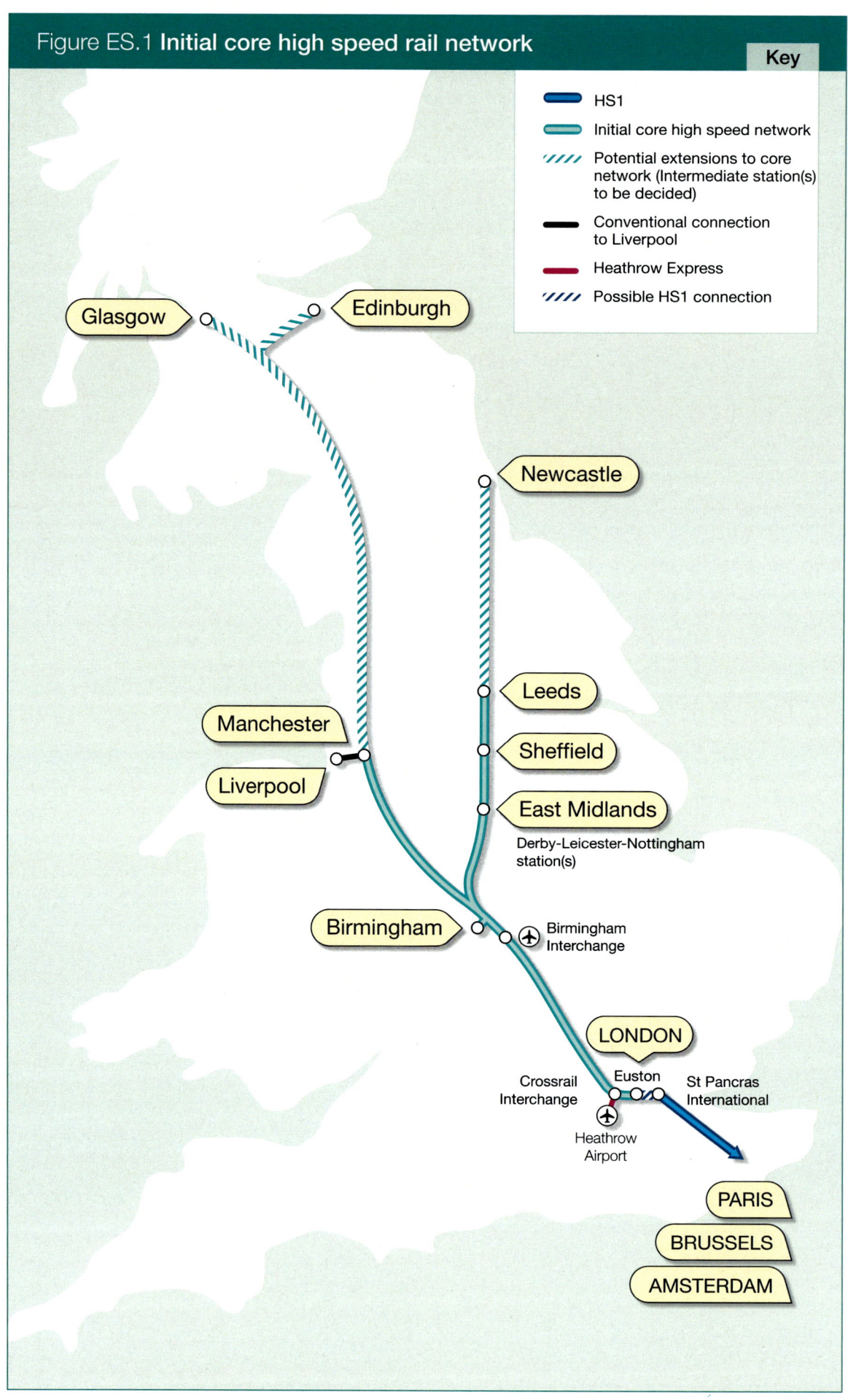

Figure ES.1 Initial core high speed rail network

The benefits of this initial Y-shaped network would not be limited only to travellers from the four cities directly situated on the high speed line. By including stations in the East Midlands and South Yorkshire, connectivity and capacity would be increased to other key cities and regions. Additional destinations, including Liverpool, Newcastle, Glasgow and Edinburgh, would be reached directly by high speed trains from the outset, by building in the links necessary for trains to continue at conventional speed onto the East and West Coast Main Lines.

Capacity

The most significant capacity benefits of this network would be felt on the three principal rail corridors heading north from London, and particularly the critical London-West Midlands corridor, whose rail capacity would be more than trebled. This would address the substantial demand growth expected on these key strategic routes, which serve extensive long distance, commuter and freight markets, as well as providing the foundation for journeys to a wide range of destinations further north, on both sides of the Pennines.

The very high capacity of the new line would be achieved both through its dedicated use for high speed operations, allowing an intensive service pattern, and through the use of longer (and larger) trains of up to 400 metres (compared to the current 207-metre Pendolinos currently in service on the West Coast Main Line).

By transferring long distance services to the high speed line, significant amounts of capacity would also be released on the existing West Coast Main Line for commuter and freight trains, including services to key areas of housing growth around Milton Keynes and Northampton.

A Y-shaped core high speed rail network yields similar increases in capacity on the East Coast and Midland Main Lines. Long-distance services to the East Midlands, South Yorkshire and Leeds would switch to the new network, as well as the southern portion of journeys to Newcastle and Edinburgh. All these lines are expected to experience significant capacity constraints over the next 20 to 30 years.

Connectivity

This initial core high speed rail network would not only provide capacity benefits, but would also significantly reduce journey times between all of the UK's largest conurbations.

The fastest journey from the West Midlands to London would be more than halved to around half an hour, and Manchester and Leeds would be brought within around 75 minutes of London, with travel time from these cities to Birmingham halved to just 40-45 minutes. The time needed to travel from Sheffield to London could be cut by 55 minutes to just 75 minutes, and from Sheffield to Birmingham from 75 minutes to just 45 minutes.

Furthermore, the links from the core high speed network onto current inter-city lines would see greatly improved connectivity to Liverpool, Newcastle, Edinburgh and Glasgow. A journey time from Glasgow and Edinburgh to London of just

3 hours 30 minutes could be achieved – fast enough to be an attractive and viable alternative to travelling by air. The use of flexible rolling stock, able to run on both high speed and conventional lines, would ensure that these wider benefits were delivered from the outset.

The connectivity benefits of this core network would be multiplied by a fast, convenient link onto Crossrail, the rapid and frequent east-west underground line through London due to open from 2017. A high speed rail/Crossrail Interchange station, west of Paddington, would slash end-to-end journey times to key destinations in the West End, Canary Wharf and the City of London. The journey time from Leeds' financial services sector to Canary Wharf, for instance, would be as little as an hour and a half.

A Crossrail interchange station would also transform connectivity between the north-south rail network and both Heathrow and the Great Western Main Line. This would bring Heathrow Airport to within an hour of the centre of Birmingham, and around 45 minutes of Birmingham Airport, and provide swift connections for those travelling to the cluster of technology and other firms in the Reading/M4 corridor, and to Bristol, South Wales and the South West. A second interchange station close to the National Exhibition Centre could bring Birmingham Airport closer to London.

Sustainability

The capacity and connectivity benefits of high speed rail are substantial. But for a British high speed rail network to be a viable way forward, it is equally important that it is sustainable.

HS2 Ltd has carried out a thorough assessment of high speed rail's potential carbon implications (based on a London to Birmingham line). Its conclusion is that, even allowing for the additional demand for travel that such a line would generate, they are likely to be broadly neutral: a change in average annual emissions in a range from -0.41 to +0.44 million tonnes, equivalent to just +/-0.3 per cent of current annual transport emissions. There would also be some carbon emitted as a result of construction but this would not be significant in the context of the UK's overall emissions.

The great majority of transport carbon emissions – around 90 per cent – are generated by road transport, and cutting these emissions will be the key factor in ensuring that the transport sector plays its full part in meeting the UK's statutory carbon reduction targets. The Government's low carbon transport strategy sets out a routemap to achieve this. Any new high speed network would also need to be designed and built to be resistent to the unavoidable impacts of climate change.

A high speed rail network would have other implications for sustainability as well as its carbon emissions. The Government is mindful of its responsibilities to protect landscapes and biodiversity, including sites of particular beauty or scientific interest, as well as to ensure that land take, noise and other impacts on local communities are proportionate.

In contrast to carbon emissions, these effects are heavily dependent on the detailed route chosen and mitigation measures deployed. HS2 Ltd has assessed a range of route options between London and Birmingham for sustainability, and identified a recommended route whose impacts on the local environment and communities are assessed as being the most consistent overall with the Government's sustainable development objectives. However, having assessed the recommended route in detail, the Government believes that further mitigation may be possible, and has asked HS2 Ltd to consider the options for providing such additional mitigation.

The Government's view

The Government's view is that the UK's initial core high speed rail network should consist of a Y-shaped network connecting London directly with Birmingham, Manchester and Leeds at speeds of up to 250 miles per hour.

The necessary interchange stations and links to the conventional rail network should also be provided to reach the full range of potential destinations from the outset, and the capacity released on existing lines should be used to expand commuter and freight services, with particular benefit for key areas of housing growth around Milton Keynes and Northampton.

This assessment will be subject to the results of the further work by HS2 Ltd that the Government has commissioned on the detailed route options and business case for the lines to Manchester and Leeds, as well as to the outcome of forthcoming public consultation.

In the longer term, the initial core 'Y' network could also provide the foundations for a more extensive network of high speed lines encompassing other English regions, Scotland and Wales. The work carried out by HS2 Ltd indicates a potentially strong business case for lines extending to Glasgow and Edinburgh, but further work will be required to understand the costs and benefits of each link in more detail and to identify the optimum solutions and funding packages. Any future decision on the construction of new lines in Scotland would be a devolved matter.

'High Speed Two' – London to Birmingham (Chapters 5 and 6)

The practical implementation of high speed rail remains a major planning, construction and funding challenge. This is why, as well as considering the options for a British network, HS2 Ltd was also commissioned to develop a costed and buildable proposal for a high speed line from London to Birmingham, 'High Speed Two', and to assess its costs and benefits.

After evaluating a range of possible station and route configurations, HS2 Ltd identified a recommended route option which their calculations indicate would deliver significant benefits of well over £2 for every £1 spent.

The Government has carefully assessed the various route options considered by HS2 Ltd, including routes using elements of the existing transport corridors of the M1, M40, A413 and West Coast Main Line, and also those which follow new alignments, for instance crossing the Hughenden Valley through the Chiltern Hills.

It agrees with HS2 Ltd that its route option 3, which in part follows the A413 corridor, appears to best meet the Government's objectives for minimising journey times and cost, and managing impacts on the local environment and communities in an acceptable way. After thorough consideration, the Government has come to the overall view that all of the other route options presented by HS2 Ltd are significantly inferior. It is therefore HS2 Ltd's recommended route option 3 which the Government proposes to put forward for public consultation in the autumn, following the completion of further work on mitigating specific impacts on the local environment and communities along the route.

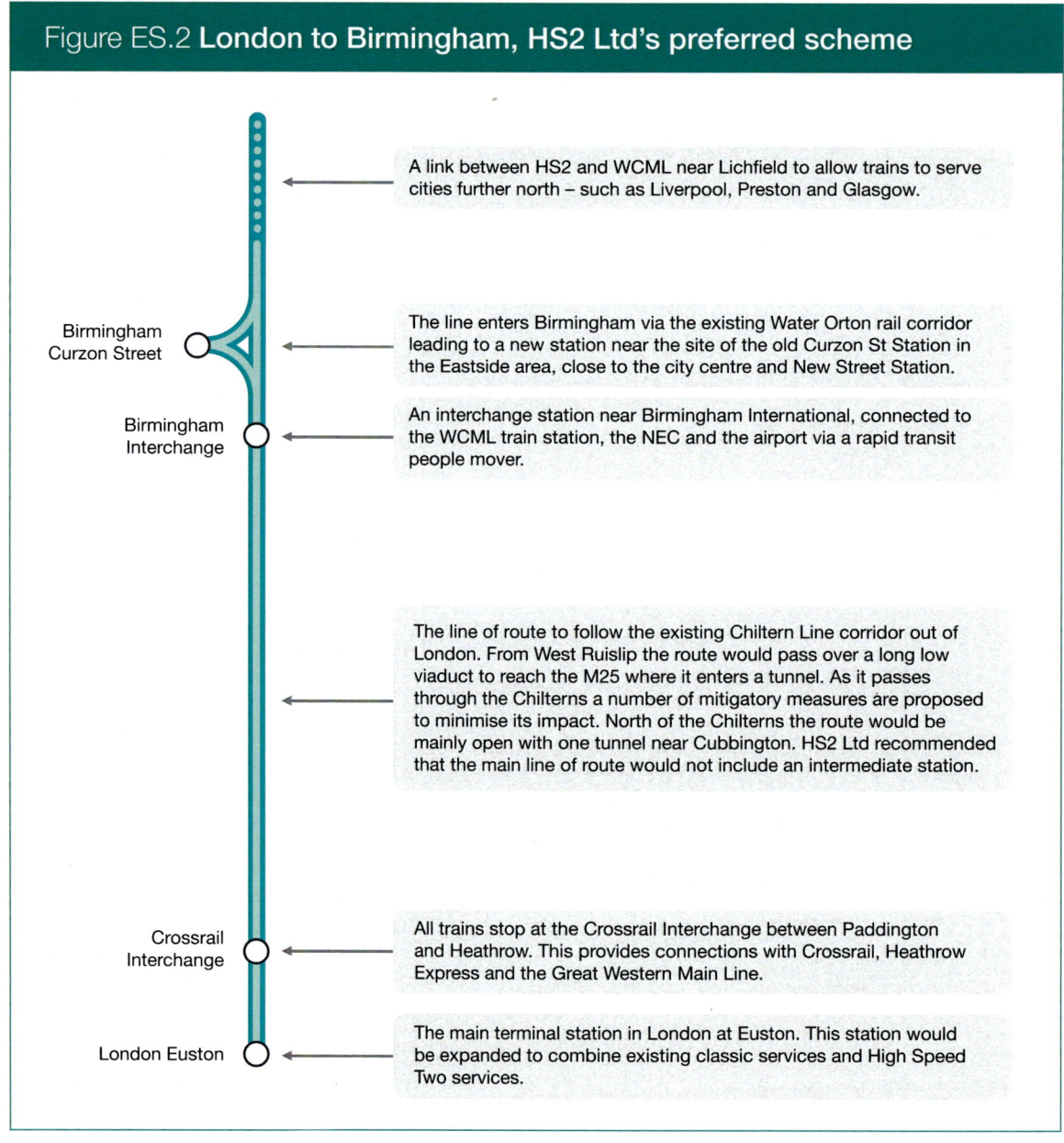

Figure ES.2 **London to Birmingham, HS2 Ltd's preferred scheme**

- A link between HS2 and WCML near Lichfield to allow trains to serve cities further north – such as Liverpool, Preston and Glasgow.
- Birmingham Curzon Street: The line enters Birmingham via the existing Water Orton rail corridor leading to a new station near the site of the old Curzon St Station in the Eastside area, close to the city centre and New Street Station.
- Birmingham Interchange: An interchange station near Birmingham International, connected to the WCML train station, the NEC and the airport via a rapid transit people mover.
- The line of route to follow the existing Chiltern Line corridor out of London. From West Ruislip the route would pass over a long low viaduct to reach the M25 where it enters a tunnel. As it passes through the Chilterns a number of mitigatory measures are proposed to minimise its impact. North of the Chilterns the route would be mainly open with one tunnel near Cubbington. HS2 Ltd recommended that the main line of route would not include an intermediate station.
- Crossrail Interchange: All trains stop at the Crossrail Interchange between Paddington and Heathrow. This provides connections with Crossrail, Heathrow Express and the Great Western Main Line.
- London Euston: The main terminal station in London at Euston. This station would be expanded to combine existing classic services and High Speed Two services.

As described by HS2 Ltd, this route would run in tunnel from a rebuilt Euston Station, surfacing in West London to follow the route of the existing Chiltern Line, leaving London near Ruislip. The route would proceed largely in tunnel from the M25 as far as Amersham, and then continue to the west of Wendover and Aylesbury, partly in tunnel and partly following the existing A413 and Chiltern Line corridor.

The next section of the route would make use of the largely-preserved track-bed of the former Great Central Railway, before continuing north west through Warwickshire to enter Birmingham close to Water Orton. The route would terminate at a new city centre station built at Curzon/Fazeley Street in Birmingham's Eastside regeneration area, with the main line extending north to join the West Coast Main Line near Lichfield, enabling services to continue at conventional speeds to destinations further north.

The Government's view is that a London-Birmingham route along these lines is viable, subject to further work on reducing the local impacts on landscape and communities, and could offer high value for money as the foundation for the high speed network. Following the completion of this work, public consultation will begin in the autumn of 2010.

Alongside this, the Government has also commissioned HS2 Ltd to undertake more detailed work on potential routes from Birmingham to Manchester and Leeds. This will be completed by summer 2011, with a view to consulting the public early in the following year.

Integration with urban and international networks (Chapters 6 and 7)

No effective high speed line can exist in isolation. Travellers are not interested in getting merely from one city centre station to another but in making complete journeys. It is therefore vital that high speed lines are well integrated with other transport networks, so that time savings are not dissipated through slow, unreliable or non-existent connections.

HS2 Ltd's modelling indicates that by far the largest market for High Speed Two would be for travellers to and from London, who would comprise more than 80 per cent of High Speed Two's passengers. As a result, the most important interchanges must be with London's current and planned urban transport networks, in particular the Underground and the new Crossrail line to be opened from 2017.

Whilst the proposed terminus at Euston would allow convenient transfer for passengers to the Victoria and Northern Lines, as well as access to other lines at Euston Square, it would not provide any connection with Crossrail. Furthermore, the large numbers of additional passengers generated by a new high speed line could cause significant operational problems on Euston's increasingly crowded Underground platforms.

A Crossrail Interchange station a short distance west of Paddington, as recommended by HS2 Ltd, addresses these issues directly. An interchange station would provide a fast, direct link to Crossrail for passengers travelling onwards to the West End, the City and Canary Wharf, enhancing the connectivity of the high speed line and significantly reducing crowding and dispersal issues at Euston.

The Government therefore agrees with HS2 Ltd's recommendation that a Crossrail interchange station is important for integration with London transport networks and should form part of the London-Birmingham line.

The Government also considers that rail access to Heathrow is an important factor for High Speed Two, given the airport's strategic importance for the UK economy.

The Crossrail Interchange could provide a rapid (around 10-minute) and frequent service to Heathrow via the Heathrow Express and Crossrail.

A strategic case has been suggested for an at-airport station in addition to, or in place of, the Crossrail Interchange. The far greater connectivity and dispersal benefits of the Crossrail Interchange have led the Government to discount the option of an at-airport station substituting for this Interchange. However, consistent with paragraph 57 of its 2009 Decision on Adding Capacity at Heathrow, the Government wishes to assess further the case for an additional high speed station at Heathrow, on a loop line from HS2 Ltd's recommended route, subject to the considerations set out in Chapter Seven. The Government has appointed Lord Mawhinney to undertake this assessment and to provide advice to Ministers.

Heathrow is not the only airport whose customers might make use of any high speed network. HS2 Ltd's report also recommends that a second interchange station should be built close to the National Exhibition Centre, providing direct access to Birmingham Airport as well as to the West Coast Main Line and the M42 and M6. The Government agrees that such an interchange has great potential to support wider connectivity within the West Midlands area and should be included as a part of the core project, subject to an acceptable funding proposal supported by the major beneficiaries. As part of its detailed design work for the routes north of Birmingham, HS2 Ltd will evaluate the business case and options for a similar interchange providing access to Manchester Airport on similar terms.

Links between High Speed Two and the existing High Speed One line to the Channel Tunnel and the wider European high speed rail network are also an important consideration. This could be achieved by a direct rail connection and/or more efficient connections from Euston to the existing High Speed One terminus at St Pancras. HS2 Ltd's report considers options for a possible High Speed Two/High Speed One link, and a short dedicated rapid transit system between Euston and St Pancras. The Government wishes to assess firm proposals for both options, and has asked HS2 Ltd to undertake further work on both, including an assessment of their business cases, prior to the commencement of consultation.

Funding a UK High Speed Rail Network (Chapter 11)

HS2 Ltd estimates the total development and construction costs of the proposed initial core 'Y' network to be in the region of £30 billion, including risk, spread out over twenty years or more. Many of these costs, and especially the very significant expenditure on construction, would not be incurred for several years. Construction would not start until after the Crossrail scheme is completed from 2017. Moreover, as Crossrail and other major capital projects such as the Olympic Park indicate, the average rate of expenditure during construction of around £2 billion per year is not unprecedented.

It is vital that any project of this scale is delivered in such a way as to provide the best possible value for money. For this reason, the Government proposes that further work should now take place on both the costs and funding options for high speed rail.

As part of its work HS2 Ltd made a comparison of UK rail engineering costs and those in comparable European countries. This work identified significant disparities – in line with the high prices that can be seen across the UK civil engineering sector. The Department for Transport and Infrastructure UK (IUK) will work together to consider how and whether the cost of relevant civil engineering works could be lowered, taking into account HS2 Ltd's evidence. HS2 Ltd will engage closely as this work progresses, and its construction cost estimates will be kept under review in the light of the results emerging from this work and subsequent actions.

In funding a new core high speed network, the Government is determined that fair contributions should be made to the overall funding package by those who will benefit from it. The Government will therefore further consider the funding options for a high speed rail network in the UK. These may include third party contributions, including developer contributions linked to new station and interchange sites, and local authority funding where the project supports local economic growth.

New Industry, New Jobs (Chapter 12)

A long-term programme of investment in high speed rail would present significant new opportunities for British business and enable the UK to capitalise on its strengths in design, engineering, construction and manufacturing.

The UK's rail sector is recognised across the world as a source of innovative products and services, from sophisticated low-carbon technologies, to engineering solutions, consultancy and major infrastructure projects. The UK has a strong and highly competitive export capability in this sector, and its open market and strong business environment make it an attractive location for inward investment.

A commitment to invest in high speed rail would provide the construction and engineering industries in Britain with a predictable, long-term pipeline of major infrastructure projects, following the completion of the current works on the Crossrail and Thameslink schemes and the Olympic Park. HS2 Ltd has estimated that the construction of a new high speed line over seven years could generate as many as 10,000 new jobs, and provide significant opportunities for the development of the UK's skills base. It would also promote the UK supply chain across the world, by providing a show case for its world class expertise across a range of sectors.

The Government will work closely with HS2 Ltd and with industry to maximise the business opportunities associated with the development of a British high speed rail network. In doing so, it will seek to ensure that firms in the UK have the skills and capability to compete successfully for contracts and to offer the best value for money, and that every opportunity is taken to promote the expertise and innovation of British firms to the broader global market.

Engagement and Public Consultation (Chapter 9)

This document describes the Government's response to HS2 Ltd's recommendations for a high speed rail line from London to the West Midlands. It also sets out the Government's proposals for a core high speed rail network extending to Manchester and Leeds, with through services running beyond, which could be developed and delivered over the next twenty years.

Transport proposals of this scale and complexity can only be taken forward through a process of full and open public engagement with those who will be affected by them and interested in them.

HS2 Ltd has been asked to carry out further work on specific aspects of its recommended route. Subject to completion of that work, the Government proposes to undertake a formal public consultation in the autumn. This consultation will cover three key issues:

- HS2 Ltd's detailed recommendations for a high speed line from London to the West Midlands.
- The strategic case for high speed rail in the UK.
- The Government's proposed strategy for an initial core high speed rail network.

Alongside this, HS2 Ltd will also develop detailed plans for extensions to Manchester and Leeds for public consultation.

Subject to the results of those consultations and further detailed work on costs and funding to feed into decisions to be taken in the next Spending Review, the next step will be to carry out the necessary preparations, including the process of environmental impact assessment, for the introduction of a Hybrid Bill for a core high speed network linking London to Birmingham, Manchester and Leeds.

This could see the London-Birmingham route opening by the end of 2026, with the legs to Manchester and Leeds opening over the succeeding years, although that is clearly dependent on securing Parliamentary approval.

But the very next step must be to ensure that the public is properly informed and to engage with local authorities and representative groups with a view to ensuring that the public consultation can be as effective as possible. The Government's plans for that process of public engagement are set out in detail in Chapter 9.

A new high speed rail network would be a project spanning the coming decades and which could transform the capacity, connectivity and sustainability of inter-urban travel in Britain. If such a network is to be made a reality, then it must be delivered in the way which best balances its potential impacts with the very considerable benefits for the UK economy and society that it would bring.

Part 1: The Case for High Speed Rail

Japanese Shinkansen ('bullet train') in Hikari Station, 1965. One of these bullet trains – long out of service – is now an exhibit in the National Railway Museum in York.

1. The Twenty-First Century Transport Challenge

1.1 Throughout the past three hundred years, improvements to transport networks have both promoted and responded to economic growth.

1.2 The canal networks created in the eighteenth century supported the first flourishing of a modern manufacturing sector by enabling the safe and affordable transit of raw materials and finished goods, for instance to and from the foundries of Shropshire and the West Midlands or the Staffordshire potteries.

1.3 In the nineteenth century, the railways improved still further the speed and flexibility with which goods could be carried. They fuelled a huge leap in productivity by permitting reliable inter-urban business travel for the first time and by transforming labour markets. The development of the railway network in Britain effectively created the concept of commuting, and in doing so contributed to the explosion in metropolitan economic activity in Victorian and Edwardian Britain, fostering trade and enterprise.

1.4 Similar patterns can be discerned in the twentieth century. The growth of motoring from the early years of the century transformed the flexibility, affordability and quality of journeys – leading to greater willingness to undertake journeys of all kinds and boosting economic prosperity and quality of life.

1.5 These benefits were further enhanced from the 1960s by the development of the motorway network, which transformed the speed and reliability of journeys between the major towns and cities of Britain. In contrast to the unplanned and unmanaged approach to railway development in the Victoria era, which bequeathed a legacy of duplication and inconsistency, the creation of the motorway network was underpinned by clear strategic planning on the part of the Government from the start. As early as 1943, the War Cabinet's Reconstruction Problems Committee considered proposals for a future motorway network, including a map (Figure 1.1), which bears a strong resemblance to the network serving Britain today.

The Twenty-First Century Transport Challenge

1.6 This network was opened over a 32 year period, beginning with the Preston Bypass in 1959. It finished in 1991 with the opening of the final section of the M40, whose completion marked the end of the construction of major new motorway alignments. Enhancements since then have focused on delivering improved performance through targeted widening schemes. Other than relatively short stretches to ease congestion in the worst affected areas, mostly notably the M6 toll road to the north of Birmingham, no significant new additions to the network have been made in England.

1.7 Alongside the increase in car travel, the twentieth century also saw an expanding and increasingly efficient aviation sector transform the UK's international connectivity, giving access to new markets and talent from across the world. More recently, low cost airlines have transformed short-haul aviation.

1.8 But it cannot be assumed that the networks developed in previous centuries will continue to be adequate to support the UK's long term prosperity and growth. Network utilisation is constantly changing. In 1910, there were 19,889 rail route miles, today it is under 10,000. Just as the canal network was long ago superseded by other faster and more flexible forms of transport, our current road and rail networks face a pattern of rising congestion as demand for travel increases.

1.9 Each decade since the 1950s has seen the planning or delivery of additional transport capacity between the UK's major cities, and this continues today. The Government is improving network performance through upgrading existing networks and through better management measures, such as hard shoulder running on motorways. This approach is delivering substantial improvements in capacity and reliability. But over the next 20 to 30 years, as the UK economy returns to a long term pattern of growth, it is almost certain that more radical enhancements of the UK's transport networks will be needed.

1.10 Successful firms will see their workforces grow and their pools of clients and contractors broaden and diversify. Changes in technology and other opportunities for innovation will see new businesses established and new markets develop. Increasing specialisation in regional and city economies will require companies to reach further to distribute their products and services and develop their customer base. Although not all new economic activity will require new travel, the scope for videoconferencing and other technological changes to reduce the need to travel appears limited.

1.11 As the economy grows, the UK's inter-city links can be expected to see a particularly rapid rise in demand for travel, fuelled by the increasing importance of high value and high-technology sectors such as business and financial services and the creative industries, which tend to cluster in major cities. As Sir Rod Eddington noted in his 2006 study of transport and economic growth, "It seems likely that these large urban areas will be the drivers of UK growth over the next few decades."

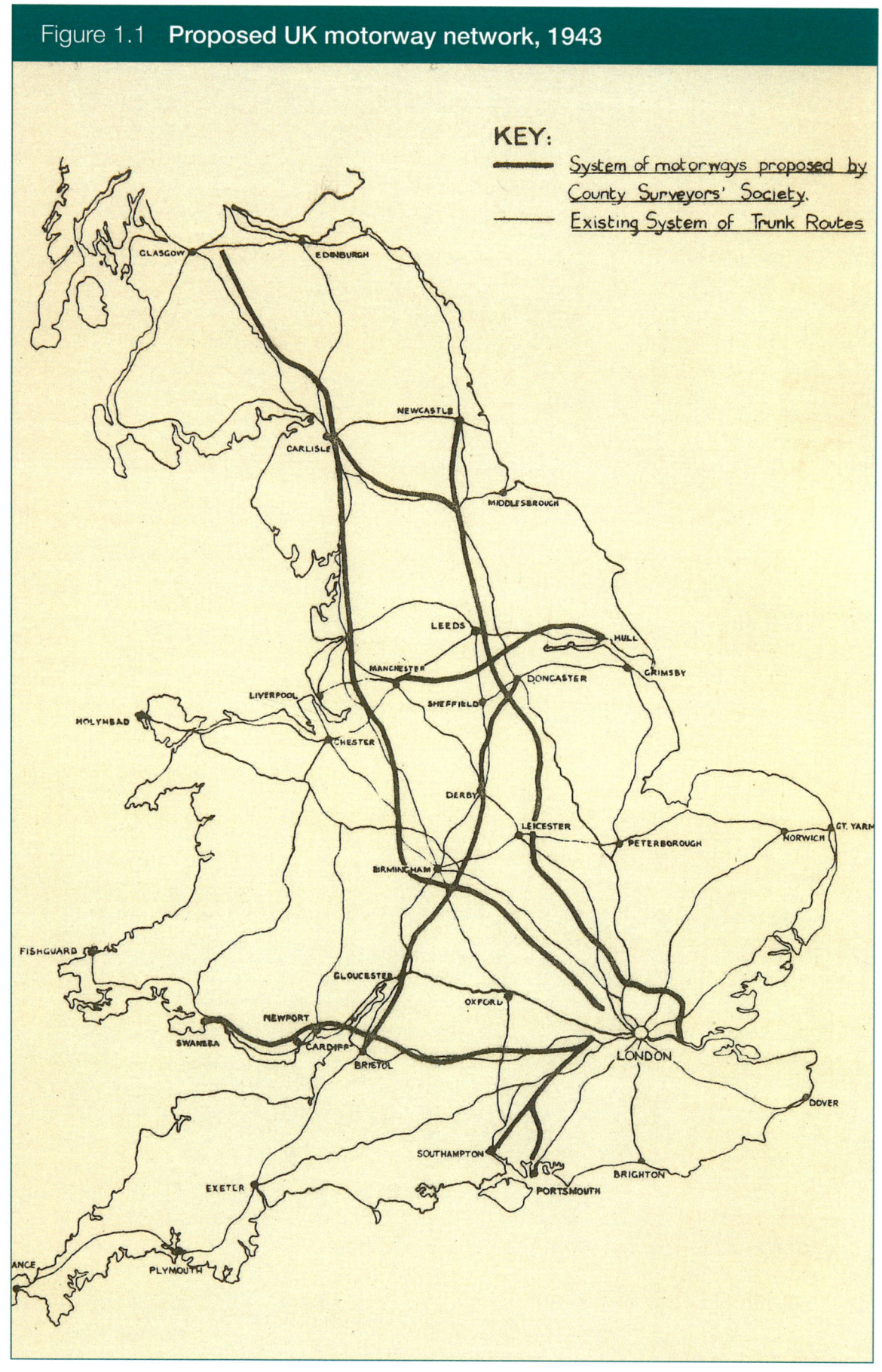

Figure 1.1 Proposed UK motorway network, 1943

The Twenty-First Century Transport Challenge

1.12 New and upgraded networks must, however, be sustainable. The Government's low carbon transport strategy sets out a routemap for reducing greenhouse gas emissions from transport through policies aimed at supporting the take-up of new technologies and fuels, promoting more sustainable forms of travel, and using market mechanisms to incentivise a shift to lower carbon choices. This strategy includes a major programme to promote the development and purchase of electric and hybrid vehicles, the electrification of the Great Western Main Line and key regional rail routes in the North West, and the entry of the aviation sector into the EU Emissions Trading System from 2012. It is vital that any measures taken to improve the capacity and connectivity of the UK's inter-city networks are consistent with this strategy.

1.13 The challenge of increasing the capacity and connectivity of inter-city transport networks whilst maintaining and enhancing their sustainability is faced by all developed countries. No other country has concluded that additional inter-urban capacity is unnecessary or unsustainable. Meeting reasonable demand for fast, convenient and sustainable inter-urban transport is seen as an imperative in maintaining long-term economic growth and competitiveness across the globe. Most other developed countries are now looking to high speed rail as a critical means of achieving this – either by expanding existing networks or by planning and constructing new ones.

1.14 For these reasons, it has been acknowledged for some time that there is a strong case for looking at the potential of high speed rail to provide a core element of Britain's future inter-urban transport network. Planning for a motorway network began some years before firm proposals reached the Cabinet. Similarly, a high speed rail network has now been given serious consideration for a decade. In 2001, the Government's Strategic Rail Authority commissioned the consultancy firm Atkins to look at the case for a high speed line from London to the North. More recently, Greengauge 21 has acted as a strong advocate for the benefits of high speed rail in the UK, while Network Rail has carried out work into the potential benefits of adding capacity to the UK rail network through both new high speed and conventional lines.

1.15 As with the development of the motorway network, however, it is for Government to take a strategic view of the case for new transport infrastructure. In January 2009, the Government took an important step forward. As part of an integrated package of measures aimed at improving the long term capacity and performance of the UK's major transport networks, including announcements on additional capacity at Heathrow Airport and a £6 billion strategic road investment programme, it published *Britain's Transport Infrastructure: High Speed Two*, which set out its proposals for analysing the case for high speed rail in the UK.

1.16 This document announced the establishment of HS2 Ltd to make a full assessment of the case for a British high speed rail network, and to develop a detailed proposal for an initial line from London to the West Midlands, reporting back to Government at the end of 2009.

1.17 This chapter explains why the Government took these steps.

The policy context

1.18 Sir Rod Eddington's 2006 transport study focused on the role of transport in sustaining the UK's productivity and competitiveness. In it, he set out a framework for transport's contribution to economic growth and identified three key priorities for long-term transport investment, which he defined as:

- the UK's growing and congested urban areas and their catchments;
- the key international gateways; and
- the key inter-urban corridors.

1.19 To meet future transport needs in these areas, he recommended that the first priority should be to focus on the performance of existing networks before considering new links, and proposed a "sophisticated policy mix" to achieve this. This policy mix was to be developed through careful assessment of the full range of policy options, including pricing, better management and infrastructure improvements.

1.20 This approach underpins the Government's current transport policy framework, which uses the full range of measures to increase capacity and improve performance and connectivity across all transport modes:

- The 2007 Rail White Paper set out an investment plan for rail to 2014, which included the completion of the West Coast Route Modernisation programme and a £10 billion programme to increase rail capacity and ease crowding, including train and platform lengthening on major commuter lines. The Government has subsequently announced plans to further improve rail performance and capacity through the electrification of the Great Western Main Line and of key inter-urban routes in the North West, new rolling stock, and a substantial upgrade of the Chiltern line.

- The recent trial of hard shoulder running at peak times on the M42 near Birmingham, together with improved real time information provision for motorists, has delivered sizeable capacity and reliability benefits. The £6 billion roads programme announced in January 2009 is rolling this approach out much more widely, alongside targeted motorway widening projects including between junctions 16-23/27-30 of the M25.

- In the UK's cities, the £16 billion Crossrail scheme and the Thameslink upgrade will transform travel into and across the capital; and the Government is also investing in a range of major urban transport schemes, including enhancements to the Manchester, Nottingham and Tyne & Wear light rail systems, at a total cost of well over £1 billion, as well as improvements to bus services, for instance through over £170 million of funding for major upgrade schemes in Luton and Cambridge.

- The 2003 Aviation White Paper described the Government's long term development plan for the UK aviation sector, including new runway capacity in the South East and at key regional airports. In January 2009, the Government confirmed its support for a new runway at Heathrow. Alongside this decision, the Government announced a target to reduce UK aviation emissions to below 2005 levels by 2050, and asked the Committee on Climate Change to assess the scope for emissions reductions from within the sector to achieve this target. The Committee's report, which was published in December 2009, concluded that a 60 per cent expansion in passenger numbers could be accommodated within the Government's targets for reducing emissions, and that for domestic and short-haul routes of under 500 miles, high speed rail could offer a viable alternative to aviation.

1.21 The Eddington study also stressed the long-term potential of road pricing to deliver capacity improvements, but the Government's view is that despite the success of the London Congestion Charge, the introduction of national road pricing is not currently technologically feasible, even if it could secure public approval. The Government will continue to assess the viability of road pricing measures for the future, keeping a particularly close eye on developments in Denmark and the Netherlands. In the meantime, more tried-and-tested means to deliver improved capacity and connectivity are required. The Government will also provide the resources, through its new Urban Transport Challenge Fund, for local authorities to pursue demand management measures if they so wish.

1.22 The Government is currently assessing the medium-term investment options for the 2014-19 period, as set out in its recent policy document, *Developing a Sustainable Transport System*. This process will allow the Government and local and regional partners to identify the highest priority transport interventions through a rigorous process of option generation and value for money appraisal.

The long-term capacity and connectivity challenge

1.23 These measures will see significant improvements in capacity and connectivity over the coming years, and will improve performance and reliability for travellers on all modes of transport. It is inevitable, however, that over the next 20 to 30 years further increases in capacity will be needed as the UK's economy returns to a pattern of long term and sustained growth.

High Speed Rail

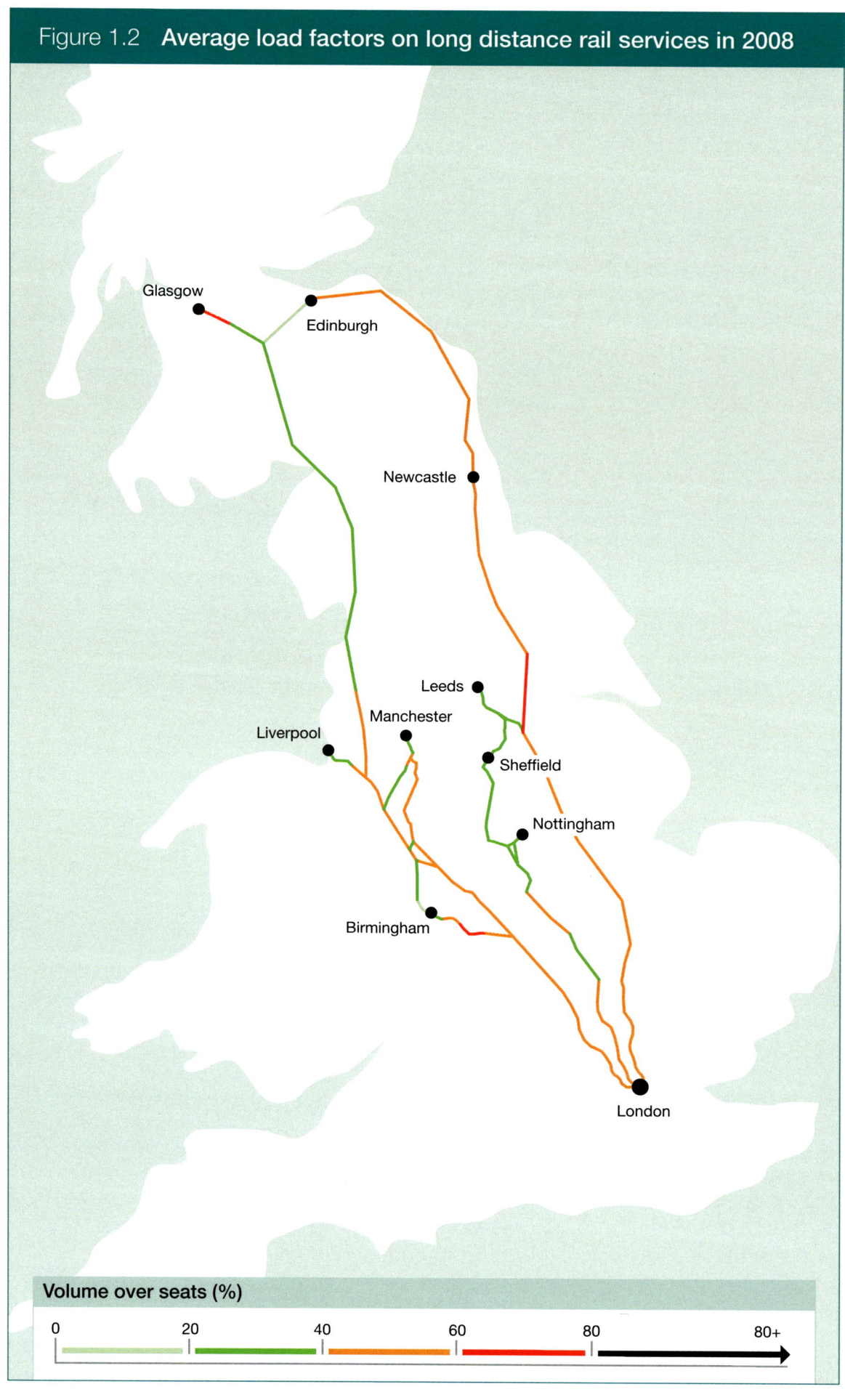

Figure 1.2 Average load factors on long distance rail services in 2008

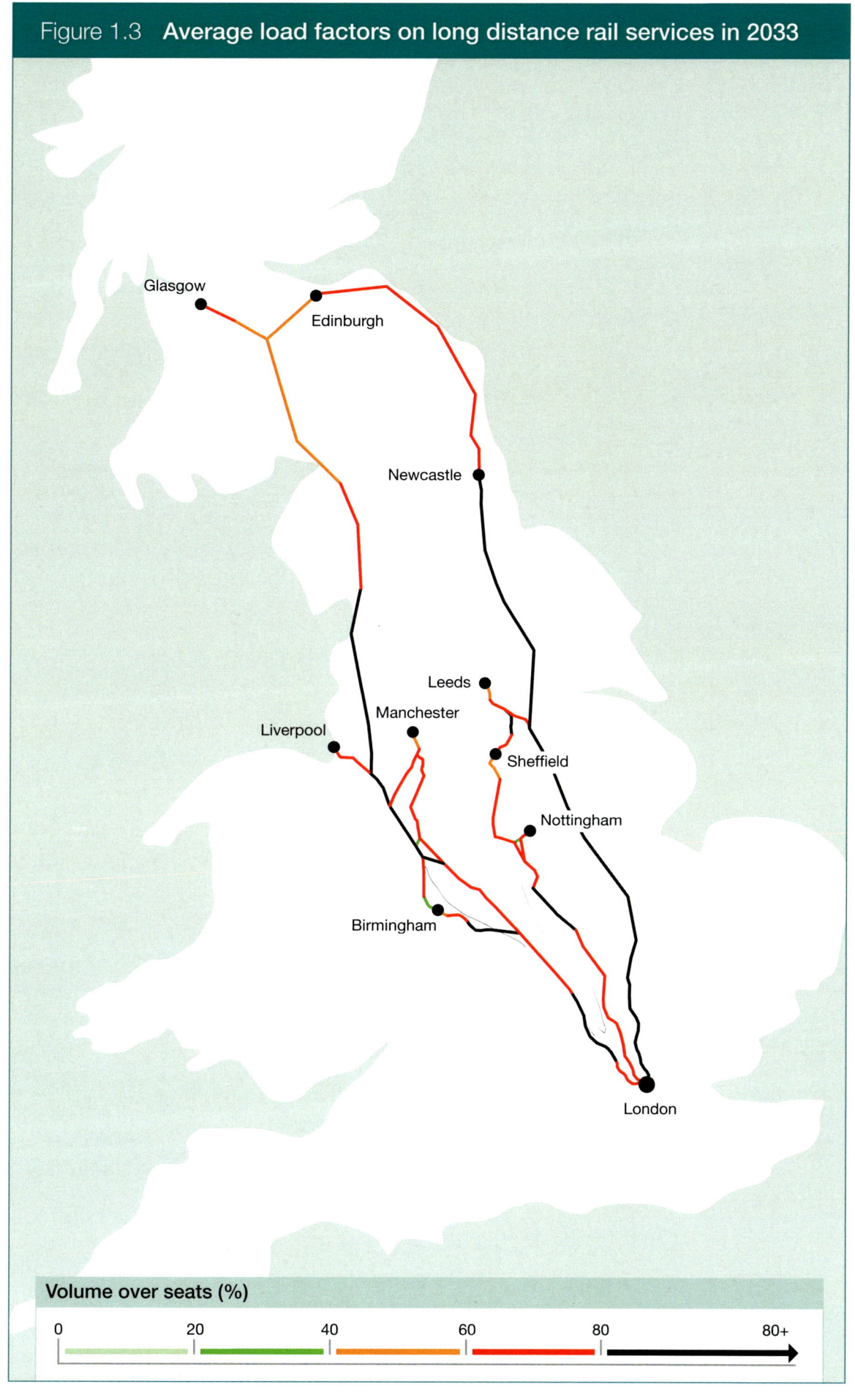

1.24 A key priority will be to improve the links between Britain's largest and most productive urban economies. This will mean, in particular, tackling crowding and congestion and improving the performance of transport links between London and the major conurbations in the Midlands and further north, where current networks are likely to be most stretched in future.

1.25 The capacity challenge is obvious. Rail journeys between these cities are already crowded at peak times and can be expected to grow ever more so unless action is taken, with crowded trains a feature for more and more of the day. Figures 1.2 and 1.3 show the increase in crowding that could be expected on long-distance services, including the routes to Birmingham, Manchester and Leeds. Peak time crowding on these routes will be even worse, routinely exceeding 100 per cent, leading to many more economically valuable journeys being forced off rail at these times.

1.26 This growing congestion on major rail lines would also have a significant impact on the freight industry and its customers. The West Coast Main Line, in particular, is a key artery for freight services, not least as it serves the UK's "golden triangle" for logistics warehousing between Rugby, Daventry and Northampton as well as several power stations and manufacturing centres. Around half of all UK rail freight uses the West Coast Main Line at some stage in its journey, including much of the UK's international and domestic intermodal rail freight traffic. The Government's modelling suggests that the vast majority of international containers using national networks between Birmingham and Manchester are on rail rather than road.

1.27 With the M6 north of Rugby carrying some of the heaviest volumes of HGVs on the motorway network, there would be considerable potential, if capacity were available, for further modal shift to rail. However, both freight customers and third party logistics providers have expressed concern that there is already insufficient capacity on the line to accommodate likely future freight services.

1.28 The motorway network is unlikely to provide an effective alternative for either passengers or freight, with congestion on the M1 and M6 increasing significantly over the coming decades, as Figures 1.4 and 1.5 show, even before the impacts of urban congestion on the reliability of city centre to city centre travel are taken into account.

1.29 Not all new economic activity will require new travel. New communications technologies have changed the way that firms and individuals work, and will continue to do so. But the scope for such changes is likely to be limited. The Climate Change Committee's recent report on aviation found that teleconferencing would reduce business air travel by only 30 per cent in their most optimistic scenario, with the net effect more likely to be close to zero, as it would be just as likely to generate additional travel (for instance, to follow up on decisions taken by videolink) than to reduce it.

1.30 As a result, the choice facing the UK will be between providing new capacity where it is essential to the economy and can be delivered sustainably, or forfeiting the economic and social benefits which growth in travel can bring.

Choosing not to provide additional capacity would be certain to lead to the regulation of demand by either price or congestion, which would tend to restrict travel to those who could afford it and which would have significant negative impacts on the UK's economy and on individual opportunity.

1.31 Improving connectivity could also provide valuable benefits for long term economic growth and prosperity. The recently completed upgrade of the West Coast Main Line has reduced journey times and improved reliability between a number of major cities. Usage of the line is increasing fast and rail's share of the overall market is growing as passengers transfer from planes and cars.

1.32 But in an age in which national and global networks of communication and interaction are constantly being enriched and expanded, public expectations about the ease and rapidity of travel will continue to rise, particularly as other countries invest in enhancing connectivity. Similarly, the global competitiveness of the UK's city economies will benefit from faster and more reliable access to the widest possible pools of skills and expertise, as well as to more extensive customer and supply bases. It will be important therefore to take every opportunity to improve the speed, comfort and convenience of inter-urban journeys in Britain.

1.33 Further investment in Britain's inter-urban transport networks will clearly be required to address capacity constraints and performance challenges in order to reduce the risk of them acting as a brake on future economic growth. Planning for such investment must be carried out well in advance of it being required, particularly if the options under consideration are to include entirely new links, as both the Eddington study and the Rail White Paper acknowledge they must, given that these can take years or even decades to plan and deliver.

The need for sustainability

1.34 Any planning for investment in Britain's inter-urban transport networks must also take account of the wider global context. The need to improve sustainability and in particular to reduce carbon emissions has gained significantly in urgency over recent years and will continue to do so.

1.35 The Government's low carbon transport strategy, published in July 2009, outlines its policy framework to ensure that transport plays its part in delivering an 80 per cent reduction in emissions by 2050, in line with the Government's statutory targets set out in the Climate Change Act 2008. This framework is based on three key approaches:

- Supporting the shift to new technologies and fuels within each mode of transport;
- Promoting lower carbon choices both within and between modes; and
- Using market mechanisms to encourage a shift to lower carbon transport.

High Speed Rail

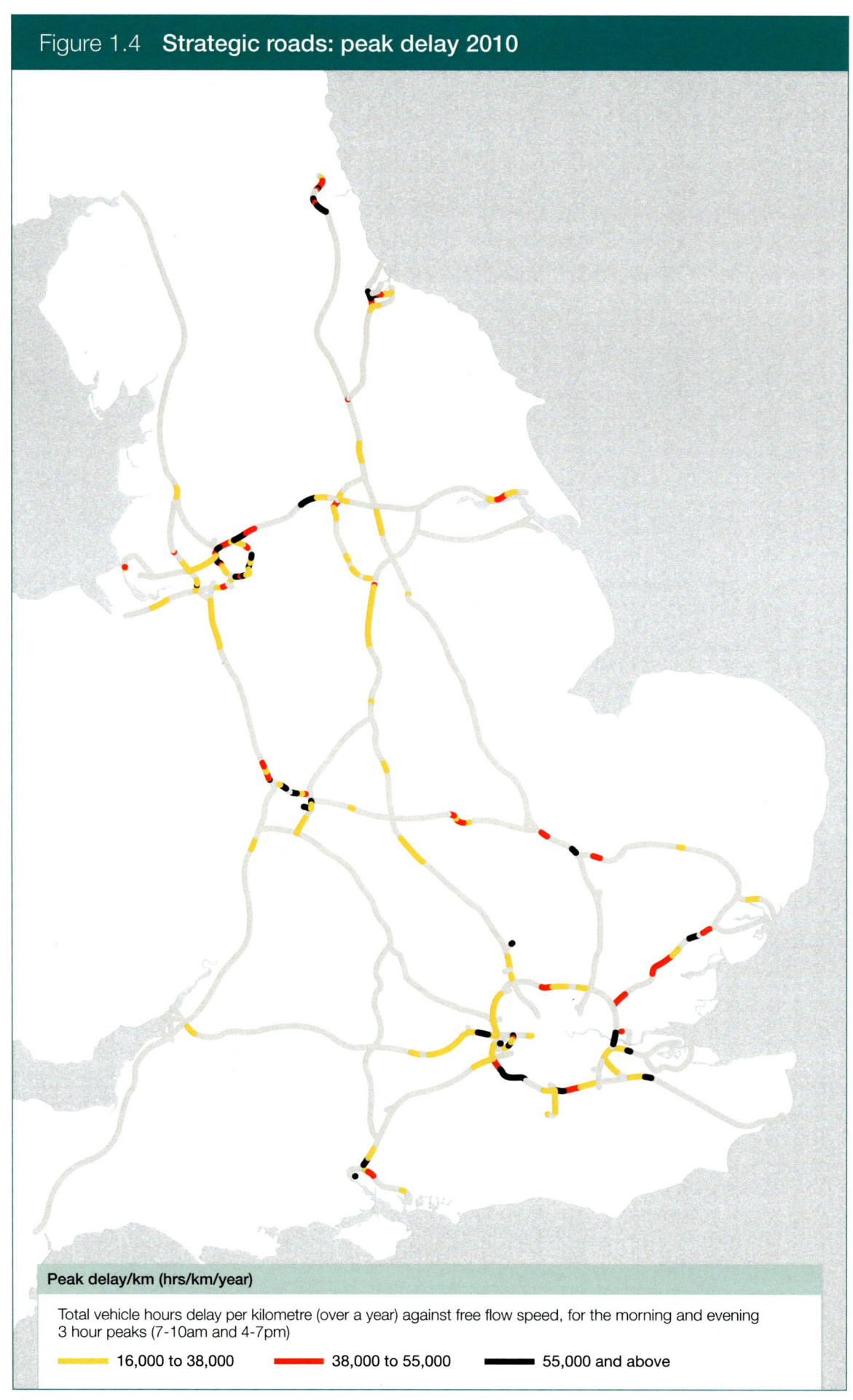

Figure 1.4 Strategic roads: peak delay 2010

Peak delay/km (hrs/km/year)

Total vehicle hours delay per kilometre (over a year) against free flow speed, for the morning and evening 3 hour peaks (7-10am and 4-7pm)

— 16,000 to 38,000   — 38,000 to 55,000   — 55,000 and above

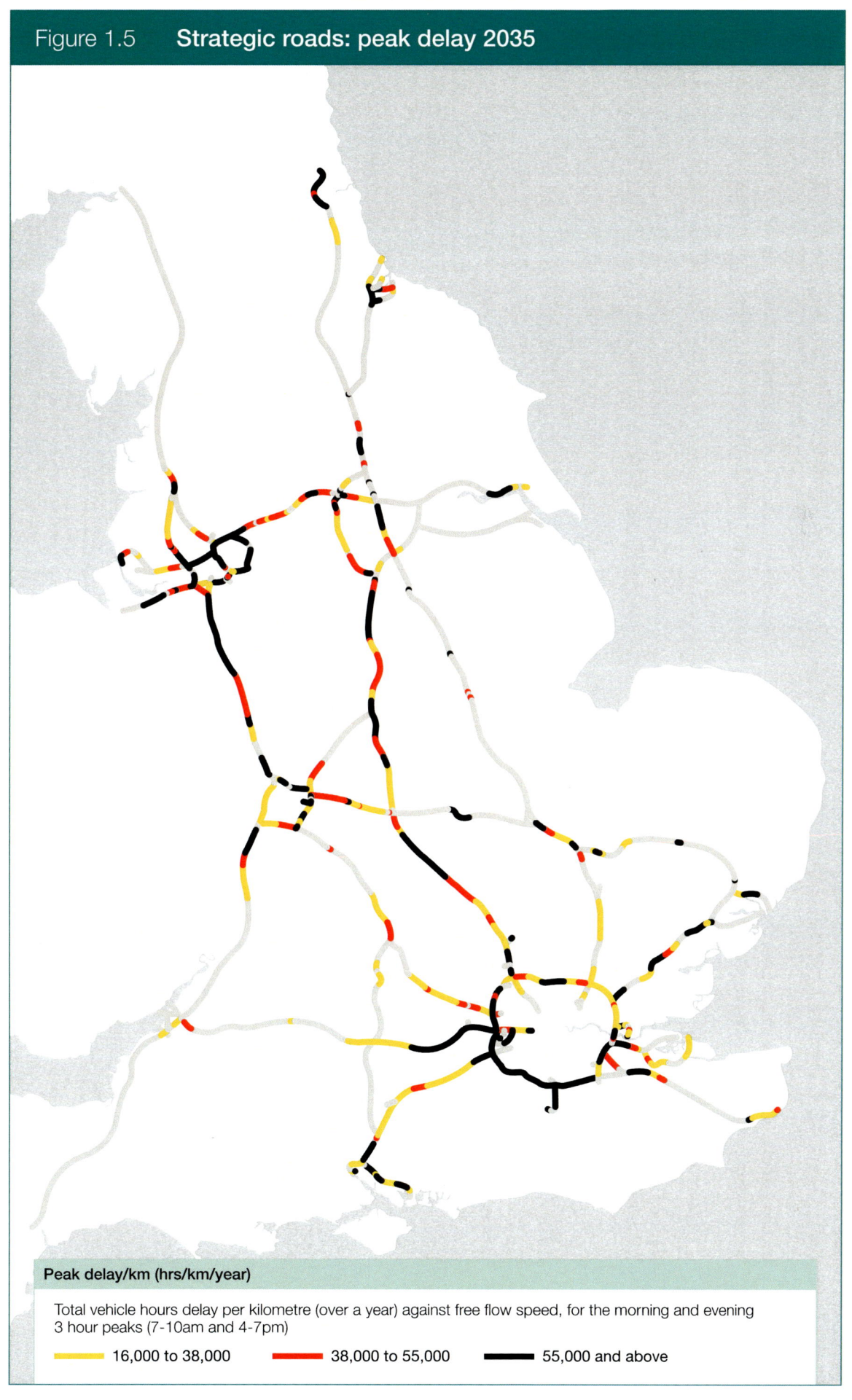

Figure 1.5 Strategic roads: peak delay 2035

1.36 Reducing greenhouse gas emissions from car travel will be a central part of achieving these goals, as the road network will continue to be the only option for many journeys. The Government is therefore investing heavily in supporting the shift to lower carbon cars, including through a £450 million programme to incentivise the purchase of electric and hybrid cars and the provision of the necessary recharging infrastructure, as well as promoting the use of sustainable biofuels and other lower carbon technologies.

1.37 Reducing the carbon emissions from rail and aviation is also important. Both the Government's 2007 Rail White Paper and the recent Committee on Climate Change report on aviation provide clear routemaps for how this can be achieved. The Government has also announced a rolling programme of electrification of key rail routes including the Great Western Main Line. It will be equally imperative to ensure that all modes of transport are effectively integrated, and that lower carbon choices are available where they are feasible – in particular for urban and city centre to city centre journeys.

1.38 Transport policy must ensure that future infrastructure is sustainable, that growth in demand is accommodated in a way that is consistent with the Government's overall carbon reduction targets, and that low carbon choices are available that will meet the changing needs of the economy and society. This must form a key part of the assessment of the options for improving inter-urban capacity and connectivity.

1.39 Any new infrastructure must also be designed, built and operated in such a way as to be resistent to the unavoidable impacts of climate change.

1.40 However, carbon emissions are not the only factor in assessing sustainability. The Government is mindful of its responsibilities to protect the natural environment, including important landscapes and biodiversity, as well as to limit harmful impacts on local communities, such as noise and air pollution, in taking any future decisions on investment in transport.

The international response

1.41 Much of Europe and Asia is looking to high speed rail to increase the capacity and connectivity of inter-city key transport networks whilst at the same time maintaining and enhancing their sustainability.

1.42 Japan was the first to introduce high speed services in 1964, with the initial Shinkansen line reducing travel times between Tokyo to Osaka to 3 hours and reaching around 135 miles per hour. The Shinkansen runs largely on a dedicated high speed network, entirely segregated from conventional lines. This network has now reached more than 1500 miles, stretching from Hachinohe at the northern tip of Honshu to Kagoshima on the southern island of Kyushu and operates at speeds of up to 185 miles per hour.

The Twenty-First Century Transport Challenge

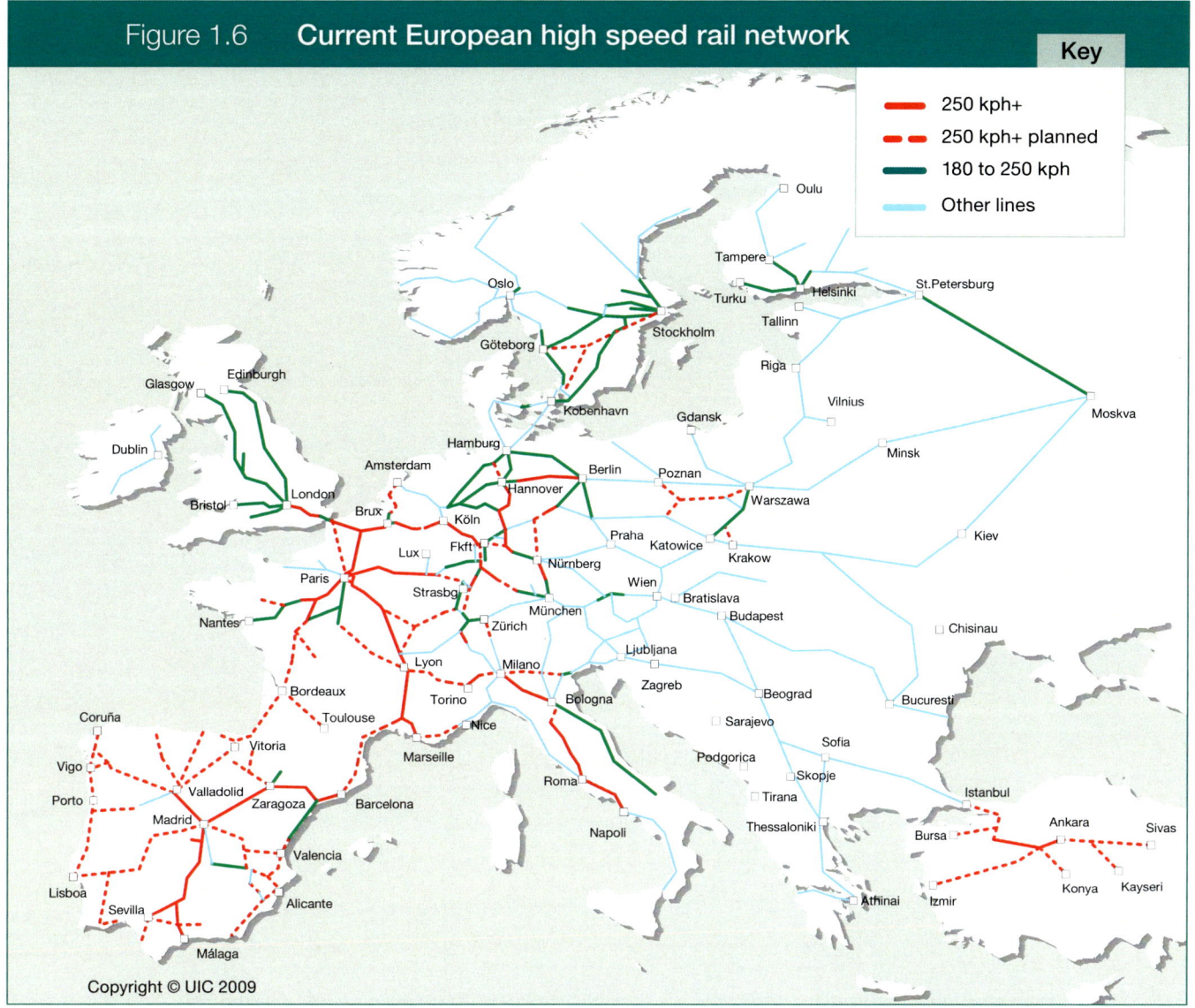

Figure 1.6 Current European high speed rail network

1.43 In Europe, although it was Italy which first completed a high speed line in 1978, France quickly established itself as the leading innovator when it opened the first *Train a Grande Vitesse* (TGV) line between Paris and Lyon in 1981. The French approach differed from the Japanese in using a combination of dedicated high speed lines and normal running on conventional lines to increase the number of destinations served, but as with Japan, the French have grown their network significantly since it opened. It now runs to over 1100 miles of dedicated high speed track, with a further 1800 miles either planned or in construction.

1.44 A wide range of European nations have now built significant high speed networks, and the rate of construction shows no sign of slowing. As shown in Table 1.1, this is matched by developments in Asia, where South Korea, China and Taiwan have joined Japan as operators of high speed services.

Table 1.1	International high speed rail networks			
Network Length (m)	Built	Under Construction	Planned	Total
Japan	1524	367	362	**2253**
France	1163	186	1626	**2975**
Spain	993	1379	1058	**3430**
Germany	799	235	416	**1450**
China	742	5611	1803	**8156**
Italy	463	82	245	**790**
Taiwan	214	0	0	**214**
South Korea	205	51	0	**256**
Netherlands/Belgium	108	97	0	**205**
United Kingdom	70	0	0	**70**

1.45 Demand for high speed rail in all these countries has been consistently high and continues to rise. Japan's Tokyo-Osaka high speed line carries over 150 million passengers per year, and in France the TGV has seen demand quadruple as its network has expanded from around 30 million journeys in 1990 to well over 120 million in 2008. In Spain, the high speed line between Madrid and Barcelona has increased rail's share of the combined train and air market between those cities from 16 per cent to around 50 per cent.

1.46 In the United States, a country with no recent track record of investing in passenger rail, the State of California's successful ballot proposition for a bond to pay the first $10 billion needed for a San Francisco to Los Angeles line has now been followed by an $8 billion programme of Federal Government funding announced by President Obama for high speed inter-city services.

High Speed Rail in the United States

The United States currently operates only one semi-high speed rail service, on Amtrak's north-eastern corridor route between Boston and Washington DC, which reaches a top speed of around 150 miles per hour.

However, the Federal Government has recognised the contribution that high speed rail can make to improving the speed, convenience and sustainability of inter-urban travel. On 28 January 2010, President Obama announced an $8 billion funding package for high speed rail projects across the United States, as part of the "largest investment in infrastructure since the Interstate Highway System was created."

The Twenty-First Century Transport Challenge

The funding will be used to support the development of 13 new large-scale high speed rail corridors, improving inter-urban links between major cities across 31 states and the District of Columbia. The map below indicates the full range of routes receiving funding.

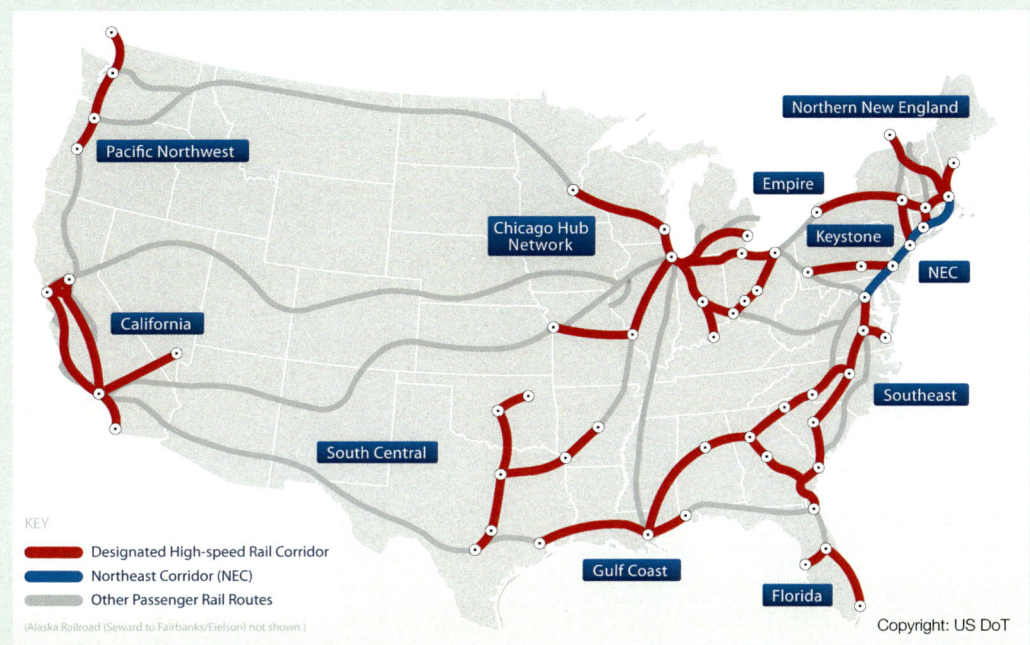

The project to develop an 84 mile high speed rail corridor between Tampa and Orlando in Florida, a little less than the distance between Birmingham and Leeds, will receive $1.25 billion in Federal funding. This line is expected to be completed in 2014 and will allow trains to run at up to 168 miles per hour, providing a journey time of under an hour compared to 90 minutes by car.

The Californian high speed rail programme will also receive significant funds. Around $2.25 billion of Federal funding will support the development of a 220 mile per hour network linking major population centres from San Francisco and Sacramento to Los Angeles and San Diego with over 300 trains per day. The journey time between Los Angeles and San Francisco will be about 2 hours 40 minutes, well under half the time it takes to make the same journey by car.

Alongside these major new schemes, additional investments will be made in a number of other States, including schemes in the north-eastern corridor, in the Midwest around Chicago, and in the Pacific north-west between Portland and Seattle.

The aims of this programme, according to US Transportation Secretary, Ray LaHood, are to improve connectivity, cut congestion, reduce emissions, and create jobs, and in doing so to "reposition America's infrastructure for the twenty first century."

From High Speed One to High Speed Two

1.47 Britain is no stranger to high speed rail. The High Speed One line from London to Brussels and Paris has cut travel times to around two hours. Rail's share of the market between London and Paris has increased to almost 80 per cent as a result. More recently, the introduction of domestic services onto the line has substantially reduced journey times into London from towns in Kent including Ramsgate, Dover, Folkestone and Canterbury, as well as from Ashford, one of the Government's key housing growth areas.

1.48 High Speed One was constructed on time and on budget; it played a key role in helping London win the 2012 Olympic Games, for which it will carry thousands of passengers an hour on dedicated Javelin services to and from Stratford; and it has restored George Gilbert Scott's St Pancras terminus to its former glory as one of the world's iconic railway stations.

> ### High Speed One
>
> High Speed One (HS1) – the 68 mile high speed line between London and the Channel Tunnel – became fully operational in November 2007. It was the first new railway to be constructed in Britain for more than 100 years. The construction of HS1 and the iconic refurbishment of St Pancras Station have been recognised with an array of awards.
>
> The new railway was an immediate success. Completion of Section 2 of HS1 – the last leg into St Pancras – which cut international journey times by a further 20 minutes, saw Eurostar passenger numbers rise 10 per cent in 2008 compared to 2007. And growth in passenger numbers continued in 2009 despite the challenging economic environment.
>
> High speed domestic services on HS1 (see Figure 3.1) commenced in December 2009. The time savings for passengers are very significant with commuters from Ashford to London having their journey time more than halved to 37 minutes. The introduction of domestic services on HS1 has released much needed capacity on the Network Rail network.
>
> HS1's performance has proved to be extremely strong with the current moving annual average of about 6 seconds delay per train from infrastructure incidents.
>
> HS1 has also delivered useful environmental benefits. An independent study found that the completion of the new line had, in its first three months, delivered a saving of 118,000 tonnes of carbon as a result of modal shift from air to Eurostar.

1.49 Similar improvements in the capacity and performance of domestic inter-urban networks will have a central role to play in maintaining the long-term economic vibrancy of the UK's major cities. It is clear from international experience that high speed rail offers a potentially sustainable means of achieving these aims.

1.50 Constructing a new high speed line would also, however, carry a significant financial cost and its impacts on the environment and local communities need to be carefully assessed to ensure that they are justified. As Sir Rod Eddington's study warned, no government should pursue a *grand projet* of this kind for its own sake or simply because a competitor city or country has one.

1.51 Therefore any future decisions on high speed rail, or other major new transport infrastructure, must be based on thorough analysis of the long term transport challenges and the potential options to address them, using the most robust evidence available.

1.52 The UK has significant experience and expertise in modelling and appraising the impacts of options to increase inter-urban capacity and performance through enhancements to the current strategic road and rail networks. But there is relatively little comparable experience with regard to new railway alignments, and the impacts of High Speed One are significantly different from those that might be expected of an inter-city network connecting Britain's major conurbations. Similarly, although the High Speed One project has provided valuable insight into the design, engineering and construction challenges involved in delivering high speed rail infrastructure in the UK, there is not the same depth of experience as there is in respect of projects to enhance existing roads and rail lines.

1.53 It was for this reason that, in January 2009, the Government established High Speed Two Ltd (HS2 Ltd), with the following remit:

"High Speed Two's purpose is to help consider the case for new high speed services from London to Scotland. As a first step, we have asked the company to develop a proposal for an entirely new line between London and the West Midlands. To reach a view on this, the company will need to assess the likely environmental impact and business case of different routes in enough detail to enable the options to be narrowed down. We expect work to be completed by the end of the year. The Government will thereafter assess the options put forward for the development of the new line."[2]

1.54 HS2 Ltd delivered its report to the Government at the end of December 2009. It is published alongside this Command Paper.

1.55 The remainder of this document sets out the Government's response to its conclusions.

---

[2] Britain's Transport Infrastructure: High Speed Two; at http://www.dft.gov.uk/pgr/rail/pi/highspeedtwo/infrastructure/

2. Capacity, Connectivity, Sustainability

2.1 In his 2006 study of transport's role in supporting economic growth and productivity, Sir Rod Eddington recommended that in taking decisions on transport investment the Government should:

> "…[enshrine] a systematic approach which starts by identifying clear objectives, takes a cross-modal approach to finding solutions, considers all types of interventions, assesses the full impacts of policies and prioritises those options which do most to deliver on [its] objectives."

2.2 The Government has carried out an analysis of the options for sustainably enhancing inter-urban capacity and connectivity.

2.3 The Government's judgement is that a viable case cannot be made for major new motorways as a sustainable solution to the UK's long term inter-urban transport needs. Nor is a significant expansion in domestic aviation considered to be a sustainable way to meet this challenge.

2.4 Therefore, a series of packages of large-scale improvements to existing road and rail networks were identified for more detailed analysis, and the costs and benefits of each calculated. The Government has reviewed these alongside the results of HS2 Ltd's comparative assessment of the case for new high speed versus conventional rail capacity.

2.5 This has demonstrated that high speed rail offers overall benefits unmatched by any other option, whilst its costs are comparable with those of alternative approaches to increasing rail capacity. The package of upgrades to Britain's current rail network necessary to deliver only half of a new high speed line's capacity benefits would be more expensive than such a new line and would be hugely disruptive to passengers and other rail users.

2.6 For this reason, the Government's assessment is that high speed rail appears the most effective way to meet its capacity, connectivity and sustainability objectives for inter-urban travel over the next 20 to 30 years.

2.7 This chapter sets out in detail how this position was reached.

Assessing the options – capacity, connectivity, sustainability

2.8 As set out in the previous chapter, the UK can expect to see demand for inter-urban travel continue to climb over the next 20 to 30 years, driven by sustained economic growth and rising prosperity, even allowing for other means of sustaining growth. Investment in inter-urban transport networks will deliver significant additional capacity. However, over the longer term, substantial additional capacity will be required to sustain economic growth.

2.9 Additional capacity must, however, be sustainable. New networks must be compatible with the Government's long term strategy to promote a low carbon economy, including its statutory targets to reduce carbon emissions set out in the Climate Change Act 2008, and their impacts on local landscapes and communities must not be disproportionate to the economic and social benefits that they would bring.

2.10 Not every option meets this sustainability test. In particular, the Government has concluded that neither a significant expansion in domestic aviation nor major new motorway alignments would be consistent with its objectives for sustainable development.

2.11 Although such a calculation will always depend on the load factors used, the evidence suggests that under most realistic scenarios the carbon emissions generated per passenger kilometre by domestic aviation will be high in comparison with other modes (Figure 2.2 sets this out in more detail). Therefore, the carbon impacts of growth in domestic aviation would be likely to be substantial.

2.12 This conclusion is in line with that reached recently by the Committee on Climate Change, whose December 2009 report concluded that whilst there was significant scope to reduce the carbon intensity of air travel over the years to 2050, this would be unlikely to offset forecast growth in full, and therefore other measures would be needed in order to keep within the Government's target to reduce total aviation emissions to below their 2005 level by 2050.

2.13 The local environmental effects of airport expansion, including noise and air quality impacts, can also be substantial. This is acknowledged in the *Future of Air Transport* White Paper (2003) which sets out clearly that the provision of additional airport capacity must be subject to meeting strict environmental criteria.

2.14 Domestic aviation will remain a viable option in some cases, particularly on longer routes – generally where the journey time for surface travel is around four hours or more – for routes from more remote destinations, and for many trips where passengers are travelling to transfer to international flights.

2.15 In respect of major new motorway alignments, the landtake and noise impacts would be a whole order more damaging than those from additional electric rail capacity. Moreover, with typical loadings, car travel is significantly more carbon intensive than even the fastest train, whilst still not matching the journey times or reliability offered by rail for city centre to city centre travel.

2.16 No major new motorway has opened since the completion of the M40 in 1991. Roads policy in England has instead focused on making better use of existing capacity and on targeted infrastructure enhancements. These have included short new stretches of motorway to relieve the most congested sections of the strategic road network, such as the M6 toll road, as well as a range of motorway widening projects and the use of hard shoulder running, which can increase capacity by up to 30 per cent without new alignments.

2.17 This is the approach to improving the capacity and performance of the strategic road network that the Government will continue to follow.

2.18 For these reasons, the Government's detailed option assessment has focused on significant packages of enhancements to the existing road and rail networks between London and the West Midlands, together with HS2 Ltd's analysis of the business case for new high speed and conventional rail lines along the same corridor. These packages, which all also take account of the Government's current investment plans for transport, are described in detail below:

Table 2.1	Rail options
Package	**Description**
Package 1	Extra long distance capacity delivered through the operation of longer trains on the West Coast Main Line (WCML) with platform lengthening and other infrastructure enhancements.
Package 2	Extra long distance capacity delivered through an increase in train service frequencies on the WCML with supporting infrastructure enhancements including extra platforms at Euston and Manchester Piccadilly stations, grade separation of junctions and 4-tracking sections of route.
Package 3	Building on package 2, the capacity and maximum speed of the Chiltern route between London and Birmingham is enhanced to allow fast WCML London – Birmingham trains to be diverted to the Chiltern Line, releasing capacity on the WCML for other services. Associated infrastructure enhancements include electrification, short new alignments, 4-tracking sections of route and additional platforms at Euston, Birmingham Moor St. and Manchester Piccadilly stations.
Package 4	Building on package 3, London – Birmingham journey times are reduced to a minimum through further infrastructure enhancements including a new alignment between the Chiltern Line and the WCML in the Kenilworth area.
Package 5	Building on package 4, additional capacity is provided between Birmingham and Stafford to enable WCML services between London and the North West to be diverted to the Chiltern route, releasing capacity on the WCML for other services. Associated infrastructure enhancements include 4-tracking the route between Birmingham and Stafford and further 4-tracking of the Chiltern route.

Capacity, Connectivity, Sustainability

Table 2.2	Road options
Package	**Description**
Package 1	Extension of hard shoulder running to the M1 (junctions 1-19), M40 (except between junctions 8 and 9) and M42 (junctions 1-7), plus widening the M42 between junctions 3 and 7 from three permanent lanes to four.
Package 2	Building on package 1, hard shoulder running is added to the M25 (junctions 15-21) – plus upgrading from five permanent lanes to six between junctions 14 and 15.
Package 3	Building on package 2, the M40 is upgraded to provide generally four permanent lanes throughout its length and five lanes between junctions 1A and 3.
Package 4	Building on package 3, where feasible, all sections of hard shoulder running are upgraded to provide a permanent extra lane.

2.19 In order to enable a robust comparison between these options and those considered by HS2 Ltd, the Government commissioned engineering firm Atkins to assess the costs and benefits of each package on the basis of detailed modelling. The following sections set out the results of that comparison in terms of capacity, connectivity and sustainability.

Capacity

2.20 HS2 Ltd's analysis shows that a new rail line connecting London to the West Midlands, and linked to the existing West Coast Main Line north of Birmingham to enable services to run on to additional destinations, would deliver a transformational increase in inter-urban capacity, potentially more than trebling total rail capacity on one of Britain's most congested transport corridors.

2.21 Any new line, whether high speed or conventional, will transform capacity. This is because:

- Firstly, any new line would in itself provide the opportunity to run very significant numbers of additional services.

- Secondly, in contrast to upgrading an existing route, a new line can easily be constructed in such a way as to permit the operation of longer trains. Current European standards for new lines require them to allow trains of up to 400 metres (in comparison to the 207 metre Pendolinos in use on the West Coast Main Line).

- Thirdly, a new line would enable faster long distance services to be segregated from slower regional and commuter services, which stop at more stations, as well as from freight. The capacity benefits from segregating service types in this way can be substantial, given that a single slower train can cut across the paths of up to seven high speed services, as the diagram below shows:

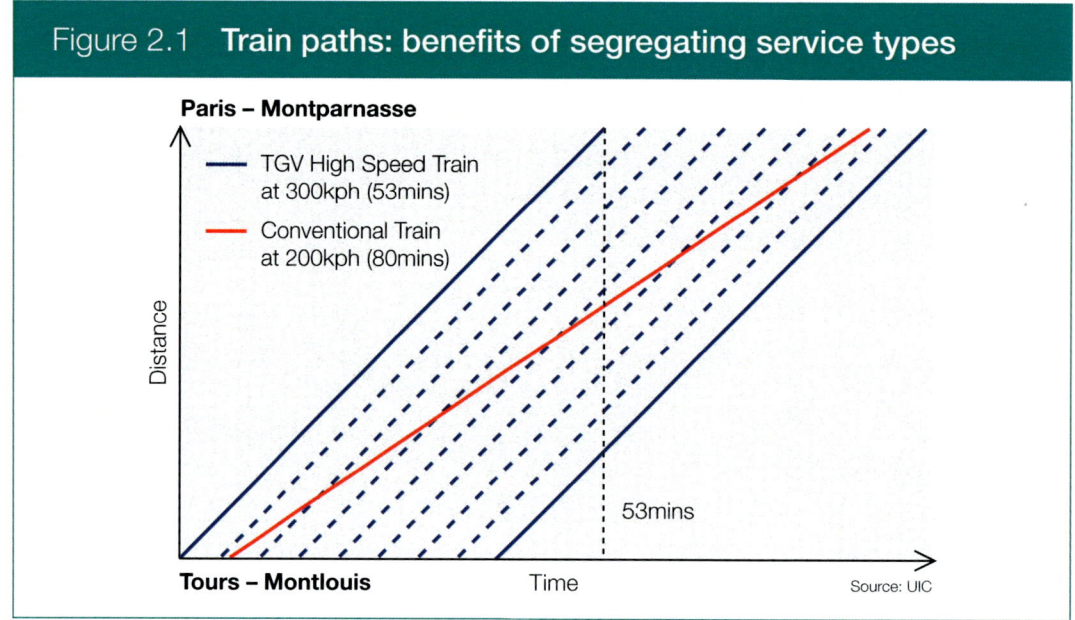

Figure 2.1 Train paths: benefits of segregating service types

- Fourthly, the use of a new line for long distance services from London to Birmingham and beyond would release significant capacity on the existing West Coast Main Line for other service types – including commuter and regional passenger trains and freight.

2.22 In contrast, works on the current rail infrastructure would not come close to matching this trebling of capacity. To deliver just half the capacity increase of a new line would require major upgrades to four important stations (Euston, Paddington, Birmingham Moor Street and Manchester Piccadilly) as well as major 4-tracking and other track and infrastructure works on the Chiltern and West Coast Main Lines. These upgrades would, taken together, cost more than a new high speed line and they would cause immense disruption to travellers over a construction period spanning several years.

2.23 In respect of the motorway options, the work undertaken by Atkins shows that further investment could provide substantial additional capacity. However, the road network is not mainly used for city centre to city centre journeys – indeed, the high levels of congestion experienced in all urban centres, and most of all in London, mean that it is generally a less reliable, and as a result less attractive, way to make such trips than rail. Furthermore, for business journeys, travelling by road provides little or no opportunity to work whilst on route, and is therefore more costly than the alternatives in terms of productivity.

2.24 Increasing motorway capacity will not solve any of these problems; it would not make city centre to city centre road journeys competitive with rail in terms of either predictability or productivity. Increased motorway capacity may be justified for other reasons – for instance, to tackle congestion bottlenecks. But it would not be an effective substitute for the direct inter-city capacity that new or improved rail lines can provide.

Connectivity

2.25 With regard to improved connectivity, the most significant benefits would clearly be delivered by a new high speed rail line, which would cut the time it takes to travel from Birmingham city centre to London by more than 40 per cent from the current 1 hour 24 minutes to as little as 40-49 minutes.

2.26 Both improvements to existing lines and a new conventional line could also provide some journey time savings, but in neither case would they be comparable with those created by a high speed line. HS2 Ltd estimates the likely savings from a new conventional line at around 20 minutes, compared to the 35 minutes provided by the high speed alternative, and the saving from a conventional line would only be delivered if it was built to a similar specification as their high speed proposal, meaning, in particular, that no stops would be included outside the two conurbations. The savings provided by upgrades to the current network would also be comparatively low – no more than 10-20 minutes at most.

2.27 In respect of new motorway enhancements, although additional capacity might improve average journey times if it effectively tackled congestion bottlenecks, it could not reduce minimum journey times. Indeed, hard shoulder running uses a reduction in speed limits as one of the measures to smooth the flow of traffic and provide more reliable journeys at congested times.

2.28 Connectivity is not only a question of the time it takes to make a journey. Improving the reliability and predictability of journeys is also a factor. Motorway improvements are of value in this respect, but these benefits would not be enjoyed in full by those making city centre to city centre journeys, as a result of the likely congestion experienced on urban roads at the beginning and end of their trips.

Sustainability

2.29 In assessing the relative sustainability of options to improve the UK's inter-urban transport links, two key issues must be taken into account: their implications for greenhouse gas emissions and their local environmental impacts.

2.30 Figure 2.2 shows the Government's estimate of the typical relative performance in carbon terms of different inter-urban travel modes.

2.31 Although the figures for aviation and rail are highly sensitive to load factor assumptions, this analysis demonstrates that, so long as a high load factor is maintained and on the basis of the fuel types currently used, carbon emissions from rail are substantially lower per passenger mile than those from other modes.

Table 2.3 UK CO_2 emissions by mode of transport			
Mode	**Total CO_2 emissions in 2007 (Mt CO_2)**	**Share of total UK domestic emissions**	**Share of UK domestic transport emissions**
Car	74.4	13.7%	55.4%
Rail	2.2	0.4%	1.6%
Domestic flight	2.3	0.4%	1.7%

2.32 Further improvements to carbon efficiency can be expected across all modes as new technologies are developed and tighter carbon constraints apply. In Japan, the most recent generation of Series N700 Shinkansen trains consumes 30 per cent less energy at 165 miles per hour than the earlier Series 0 model travelling 30 miles per hour slower. The average fuel consumption of new cars in the UK has fallen by almost 20 per cent since 1998.

2.33 In the same way, more fundamental changes to how transport is powered may occur, with significant implications for long-term carbon emissions. The electrification of the car fleet and uptake of sustainable biofuels, as envisaged in the Government's low carbon transport strategy, may over a long period of time reduce road transport's emissions per passenger mile relative to rail.

2.34 However, it is likely that the comparative advantage in terms of greenhouse gas emissions will continue to lie with rail for many decades. And increasing decarbonisation of electricity could improve rail's advantage over road in the interim.

2.35 Moreover, in the light of the UK's statutory targets for the reduction of carbon emissions, which were set in the Climate Change Act 2008, it is not enough merely to identify that rail is preferable to road in terms of *relative* carbon emissions. Having identified a preferred option for delivering enhanced inter-urban capacity and connectivity, it will be necessary to ensure that its *absolute* impact on carbon emissions is consistent with the achievement of these targets. This issue is discussed in more detail later in this chapter.

2.36 The second sustainability issue that must be taken into account is the impact of each option on the local environment, including its implications for landscape, air quality and noise.

2.37 In contrast to carbon emissions, these impacts are highly dependent on the specific route chosen and mitigation measures employed. The likely environmental impacts of any specific option must be considered in the context of more detailed planning and assessment, informed by public consultation.

Capacity, Connectivity, Sustainability

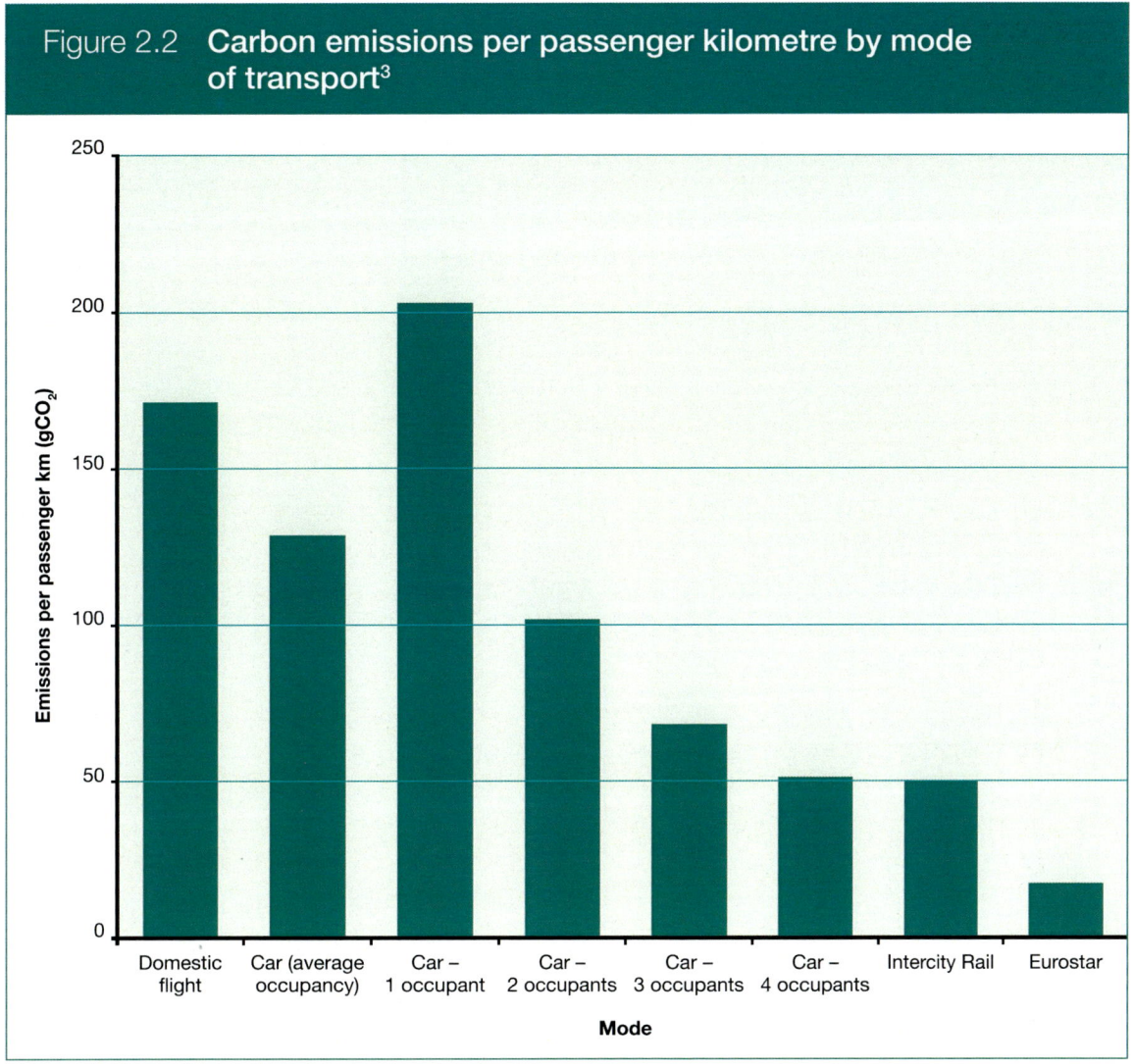

Figure 2.2 Carbon emissions per passenger kilometre by mode of transport[3]

2.38 All major transport infrastructure projects will have some negative impacts. Any new alignment, whether road or rail, conventional or high speed, will require a significant amount of land take, and railways as well as motorways will have a degree of negative impact in terms of noise. However, a new motorway would require at least twice as much land as a high speed rail line, and motorways can be harmful for local air quality, whereas new railways would rely on electric power.

2.39 In terms of completely new alignments, therefore, the environmental advantage will lie with rail. It is also likely that the impacts of new alignments will be somewhat higher than those of major improvements to existing infrastructure, though these should still not be underestimated. But in all cases appropriate detailed mitigations would need to be put in place to ensure that such impacts were managed and reduced wherever possible.

---

3 Figures for car travel, aviation and Eurostar are based on Defra's Company Reporting Guidelines (2009). Intercity rail figures are derived from the Department for Transport's network modelling framework. All figures are based on an average load factor for the mode.

The overall assessment – costs and benefits

2.40 As set out above, a new railway line would supply the greatest increase in capacity, with only a high speed line being able to add to this significant connectivity benefits. The rail options are also likely to be the most sustainable, so long as their local environmental impacts are appropriately mitigated, and usage is consistently high enough to maintain their relative advantage in terms of greenhouse gas emissions.

2.41 Overall, therefore, it appears probable that a high speed line will offer the greatest benefits: a conclusion borne out by the analysis carried out for the Government by HS2 Ltd and Atkins. This analysis was based on calculations of the economic value of the capacity and journey time improvements of each of the options, and is published alongside the Command Paper.

2.42 However, any analysis of the options must also take account of the costs of each proposal, in order to make an assessment of its overall value for money, especially given the potentially very high costs of some of the options, including not only a high speed line, but also some of the more significant upgrade packages.

2.43 Table 2.4 sets out the costs and benefits of the options considered, along with the overall value for money calculation for each one. It focuses on two of the packages considered for each of road and rail – firstly that offering the highest value for money and secondly that offering the highest benefits regardless of cost. It also includes an assessment of the disruption that would be caused by each option to travellers during construction.

2.44 The costs used in the table are the net cost to government – i.e. the overall cost less any revenue that would be generated by the project (e.g. through fares). They show clearly that the largest upgrades to existing railway lines are more expensive than an entirely new line over the long term, yet these can at best provide only half of the capacity benefits of a new line.

2.45 The net costs of a new conventional line are only marginally lower than those of a high speed line. This is because without the connectivity benefits offered by high speed rail, a conventional line would not attract the same number of passengers, and as a result its fare revenues would be significantly lower than those of the high speed equivalent.

2.46 Furthermore, it is unlikely that these calculations capture the full costs of each project, once disruption to travellers is also taken into account. The modernisation of the West Coast Main Line took almost a decade to complete. Its costs included more than £500 million in compensation to train operating companies as a result of disruption to their services, and this accounted for only a fraction of the economic and social cost of the disruption to passengers and other rail users. The larger rail upgrade packages outlined here would be on a similar scale, with similar potential impacts. Equally, the packages of road upgrades would entail significant disruption for motorists whilst construction takes place.

Capacity, Connectivity, Sustainability

Table 2.4 Comparative benefits of new capacity options, London to Birmingham

Comparison of London-West Midlands Corridor options	Mid-scale rail upgrade package	Large-scale rail upgrade package	New conventional Rail	New High Speed Rail	Mid-scale road package	Large-scale road package
Maximum potential capacity increase	~50%	~100%	~200%+	~200%+	~20%	~20%
Journey time improvement	~10 mins	~20 mins	~20 mins	35 mins	~2–4 mins	~3–6 mins
Present value costs to HMG (bn)	£3.1	£13.7	c. £11.5	£11.9	£1.4	£3.2
Present value benefits (bn)	£6.8	£11.6	c. £22.5	£28.7	£5.1	£7.0
Benefit:cost ratio	2.2	0.9	~2.0	2.4	3.7	2.2
Disruption impact	Works at Euston and Manchester Piccadilly. Grade separation and significant 4-tracking on WCML.	Works at 2 major London terminals, Birmingham Moor St. and Manchester Piccadilly. Significant 4 tracking of WCML and almost all of Chiltern Line	Major works at Euston and connection to WCML at Lichfield	Major works at Euston and connection to WCML at Lichfield	Modification of 255 motorway lane miles for Hard Shoulder Running and widening of 34 lane miles with associated temporary speed restrictions and lane closures	Widening of 448 motorway lane miles with associated temporary speed restrictions and lane closures

51

2.47 It is clear from this assessment that there are still strong gains to be made from the further roll-out of hard shoulder running. But it should be noted that the value for money offered by even the smallest and cheapest packages of measures is lower than that of the current managed motorways programme. It appears likely that the scope for incremental improvements to continue to offer high value for money is finite, with the returns from such packages decreasing substantially as they grow in size and cost.

2.48 In contrast, the benefits delivered by a new London-Birmingham high speed line are in excess of those from any other option under consideration, totalling almost £29 billion as a result of radical capacity increases and a dramatic reduction in journey times. Furthermore, even when the costs of such a line are taken into account, it offers value for money greater than that of any but the smallest packages of road improvements, providing well over £2 of benefits for every £1 spent.

Compatibility with UK's carbon targets

2.49 A high speed line would provide very significant capacity and connectivity benefits and offer high value for money as a result. But as noted in paragraph 2.35, it can only be a viable option if its carbon emissions can be accommodated within the UK Government's statutory targets for reducing overall greenhouse gas emissions.

2.50 It is therefore important to take into account not only its *relative* carbon impacts compared to other modes, but also the *absolute* increase or reduction in carbon that it would entail compared to what would happen if such a line was not built. This means ensuring a) that its emissions are justified by the wider benefits it offers, and b) that any change in emissions as a result of such a line can be accommodated within the UK's overall strategy for reducing transport's impacts on climate change.

2.51 With regard to a), the assessments of value for money set out above include carbon emissions and other environmental costs, and demonstrate that the carbon cost of a high speed line would be significantly outweighed by its capacity and connectivity benefits. Also, given that any new high speed line would rely on electric power, it should be noted that its power sources would be covered by the European Union Emissions Trading System. This means that it could not generate any net increase in emissions at the EU level, although unless renewable electricity sources were used its operators would need to purchase allowances to cover its energy requirements.

2.52 With regard to b), the overall carbon impact of a new high speed line would depend on three factors:

i) the carbon emitted as a result of construction (referred to as "embedded carbon");

ii) the increased carbon emissions as a result of high speed journeys that would not otherwise have been made (or to a lesser extent switches from conventional rail, which has lower emissions); and

iii) the reduction in carbon emissions due to some journeys switching to high speed rail from higher carbon modes such as the car and aviation.

2.53 HS2 Ltd's assessment is that the overall embedded carbon from building a London to Birmingham line is relatively small, only 1.2 million tonnes over the entire construction period, and not significant in the context of the UK's overall emissions.

2.54 Therefore, the key issue in terms of a high speed line's compatibility with the UK's statutory targets to reduce emissions is whether the carbon emitted as a result of the operation of a high speed network is consistent with the UK's carbon reduction targets.

2.55 HS2 Ltd's calculations suggest that it is. They indicate a range of potential changes in carbon emissions over 60 years resulting from a high speed line from London to the West Midlands of -25.0 million to +26.6 million tonnes, depending on the level of modal shift achieved and the rate at which electricity generation ceases to rely on fossil fuels. The basis for this calculation is set out in Table 2.5.

Table 2.5 Range of carbon impacts estimated by HS2 Ltd for a high speed line from London to Birmingham	
	Change in CO_2 over 60 years ($MtCO_2$)
HS2 Emissions	0 to +26.1
Other Rail Impacts	-1.3 to +0.5
Car Mode Shift	-0.5 to 0
Air Mode Shift	-23.2 to 0
Total	-25.0 to + 26.6

2.56 It should be noted that these figures do not assume that travellers from London to Birmingham, or vice versa, would switch from air, as the journey is too short for aviation even now. Rather, HS2 Ltd's modelling suggests that it is the journey time savings delivered to more northerly destinations, such as Manchester and Glasgow, through high speed services connecting onto the West Coast Main Line, that would encourage some modal shift from plane to train. If a wider network was built, with further reductions in journey times to Manchester, Newcastle, Glasgow and Edinburgh, the potential for modal shift and consequent carbon reductions would be far greater.

2.57 But even if no modal shift at all was achieved and there was no improvement in the carbon intensity of electricity generation, HS2 Ltd's figures still indicate that the additional carbon generated would average only around 0.44 million tonnes per year. To put this in context, this figure would represent around 0.3 per cent of current domestic greenhouse gas emissions from transport, which totalled 131.9 million tonnes in 2008.

2.58 There is plenty of evidence to suggest that high speed rail can attract passengers from aviation. Rail's share of the combined rail/aviation market increased from under 25 per cent to over 80 per cent following completion of the Madrid-Seville high speed line. Closer to home, by improving journey times and reliability for services between London and Manchester, the completion of the West Coast Route Modernisation led to roughly a doubling in rail's share of the combined market from one third to two thirds.

2.59 Even so, aviation will remain the most attractive choice for some journeys – most notably, those of more than 500 miles, such as from London to the north of Scotland.

2.60 Any calculation which relies on modal shift will be sensitive to changes in the relative carbon efficiency of each mode. But there is no good reason to believe that these changes would significantly disadvantage high speed rail. As set out in paragraph 2.32, history shows a clear pattern of increasing efficiency from high speed rail in other countries, no less than from car travel.

2.61 The Government's assessment therefore is that high speed rail is consistent with its carbon reduction targets for transport, and the option which most effectively balances its capacity, connectivity and sustainability objectives for inter-urban transport.

2.62 This should come as no surprise. Rail is a comparatively low carbon mode of transport, responsible for just two per cent of overall transport emissions. In contrast, road transport is responsible for around 90 per cent, so efforts to improve the efficiency of that sector will inevitably form the main part of any transport carbon reduction strategy.

The case for high speed rail

2.63 Chapter One demonstrated that the UK will require significant improvements in inter-urban capacity and connectivity over the next 20 to 30 years, in order to support its continued economic growth and prosperity.

2.64 The Government has considered a range of options to meet these goals. Its assessment is that high speed rail is the most effective way forward. Neither major new motorways nor a significant expansion of domestic aviation can be considered a sustainable solution to the UK's long term inter-urban transport needs. And high speed rail offers benefits unmatched by any other option including new conventional rail lines or major upgrades of existing road or rail networks.

2.65 However, it is unlikely that this would be the sum total of the benefits of such a line. Over and above its conventional transport benefits, a project of this kind could play a significant role in helping deliver increased competitiveness and productivity in the UK and supporting regional economic growth. The next chapter looks at these benefits in more detail.

3. Supporting Growth in the Regions

3.1 Chapter Two examined the case for high speed rail against other options for tackling the UK's inter-urban transport challenges over the next 20 to 30 years. Its assessment was that high speed rail is the most effective way to deliver sustainable improvements in capacity and connectivity between the major conurbations of the North, the Midlands and London. On that basis alone high speed rail appears the most attractive option.

3.2 However, the direct benefits in terms of increased capacity and reduced journey times are unlikely to be the sum total of the benefits of a high speed network in Britain.

3.3 Such a network could also provide important support for long-term regional economic growth in the UK, for instance by:

- Increasing the productivity of the UK's urban economies by providing access to deeper labour markets and wider pools of customers and suppliers as a result of faster and more reliable inter-urban journeys;

- Enabling the major cities of the Midlands and the North to compete and collaborate more effectively, particularly when combined with improvements to Trans-Pennine services. This would incentivise greater specialisation and promote investment and growth in these regions.

- Supporting housing growth in the Milton Keynes/South Midlands growth area (MKSM), through the use of released capacity on existing lines to provide enhanced commuter services; and

- Promoting London's long-term competitiveness, by providing efficient connections between urban, national and international networks.

3.4 This chapter explains these potential benefits in more detail and describes the contribution that the Government believes a high speed network could make to regional economic growth over the next 20 years as part of the UK's twenty-first century economic infrastructure.

Increasing urban economic productivity

3.5 Improving transport links has long been acknowledged as a key means of supporting growth and increasing productivity in major conurbations.

3.6 This is not only because such measures reduce journey time for travellers, but also as a result of wider effects. Increasing the distance that can be travelled within a given time broadens the pools of employees, customers and suppliers that a firm can access, and thereby enables businesses to recruit staff whose skills more closely match their requirements, to sell their products more widely, and to get better deals from suppliers, reducing the costs for their customers. It can also create 'knowledge spillovers', which incentivise skills improvements and innovation, because companies and individuals are more likely to interact with and therefore be able to gain from a greater depth and variety of contacts.

3.7 These processes – referred to by economists as 'agglomeration effects' – enhance competition and innovation, reduce costs, increase productivity and create business opportunities. They were highlighted by Sir Rod Eddington as one of the most important ways in which transport investment can support economic competitiveness, alongside the increased efficiency created by faster and more reliable journeys:

"Transport improvements can expand labour market catchments, improve job matching, and facilitate business to business interactions."

3.8 The Department for Transport has published draft guidance on valuing impacts of this kind from transport schemes, and HS2 Ltd used this to assess the potential agglomeration benefits arising as a result of their proposed London-Birmingham high speed line.

3.9 HS2 Ltd's calculation suggests that the wider agglomeration benefits related to such a line could amount to around £2 billion at 2009 prices over a 60 year period. This figure is derived specifically from the benefits of improved linkages between firms. HS2 Ltd's report also acknowledges that there could be additional benefits as a result of the new line enabling people to move to more productive jobs, but these benefits are more uncertain and have not been valued.

3.10 Furthermore, it is likely that the agglomeration benefits from high speed rail connections between other cities would also be of value – especially between Birmingham and both Manchester and Leeds, given the short distances between these significant economic centres, which are poorly connected at present. Further work will be undertaken to measure these benefits.

3.11 HS2 Ltd also identified a second wider economic benefit from a new London-Birmingham line: increased productivity generates benefits in line with the value that customers place on the goods and services that result, which tends to be higher than the costs of production alone. This benefit, calculated in accordance with Department for Transport guidance, is estimated at around £1.6 billion over 60 years.

3.12 Taken together, if these additional benefits are added to those included in HS2's calculation of the conventional benefits of a London to Birmingham line its benefit:cost ratio increases from the 2.4:1 quoted in Chapter Five to around 2.7:1.

Supporting Growth in the Regions

3.13 In order to inform their assessment of the wider benefits of a high speed line from London to the West Midlands, HS2 Ltd also commissioned research to assess the degree to which agglomeration benefits were likely to be created between major economic centres through transport improvements on major inter-urban routes. This research concluded that improved connectivity between cities could create agglomeration and other wider economic benefits, and as a result that:

"...high speed rail could have an important effect on the level of connectivity between firms (business movements) and between workers (community movements)"[4]

3.14 These effects are more uncertain than those experienced within urban centres that informed the calculations above, and they would also not be expected to be as pronounced. Nonetheless, the research indicates that there could be some additional benefits from a high speed line not picked up by the existing guidance on valuing agglomeration effects.

Supporting growth in Britain's core cities

3.15 The wider economic benefits of a UK high speed rail network might be most substantial in the major city regions of the North and the Midlands. Despite the comparatively short distances between them, rail journey times between these cities can be surprisingly high – an hour and a half for the 95-mile trip from Birmingham to Manchester, and around two hours for the similar length journey to Leeds. Rail journeys tend to be especially lengthy where crossing from one of the major Victorian north-south arteries to another, for instance from the West Coast Main Line in Birmingham to destinations such as Sheffield or Nottingham on the Midland Main Line or Leeds on the East Coast Main Line.

---

4   *Advice on the Assessment of Wider Economic Impacts: A Report for HS2*, Daniel J. Graham and Patricia Melo, 2010

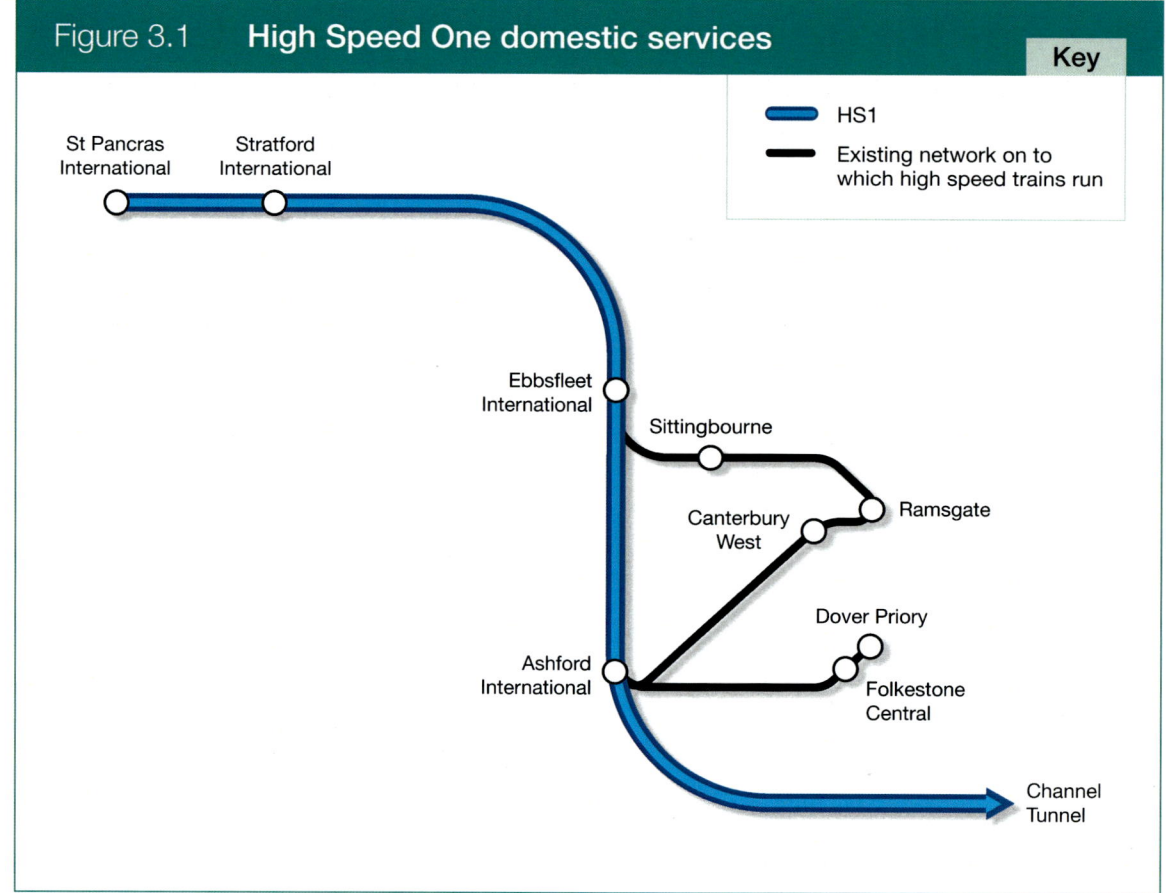

Figure 3.1 High Speed One domestic services

3.16 Furthermore, the strategic road network cannot offer a competitive alternative for city centre to city centre travel. The motorway connections between these cities are amongst the most congested motorway links in Britain after the M25 and, even when uncongested, journey times by car are as high or higher than those by rail, given the slower average speeds compared to rail and the difficulty of access to city centres.

3.17 This lack of connectivity between the major urban economies in these regions is likely to be one of the important reasons why they continue to function more as isolated economies than as a single functional economic area. This has been identified as a key weakness in research commissioned by the Northern Way into city economies in northern regions, which notes that:

"the cities of the North largely operate as relatively self-contained economic entities ... Hence, any synergy between the North's two major cities of Manchester and Leeds, which might in principle be expected to increase their potential to act together as a countermagnet to complement London and the wider South East, is largely unrealised since service industries in the two cities largely replicate each other."[5]

---

5 *A report to the Northern Way: The roles and economic functions of the city regions of the North* (2008); at http://www.thenorthernway.co.uk/downloaddoc.asp?id=458

Supporting Growth in the Regions

3.18 An initial core high speed network linking Birmingham to Manchester and Leeds, together with improvements to the Trans-Pennine routes connecting those two cities could play an important role in addressing this. By improving journey times, capacity and reliability between those cities, and potentially other major conurbations in the East Midlands and South Yorkshire, it could make it significantly easier for firms based in one city to work across these regions rather than being restricted to a single conurbation.

3.19 In the short term this could reduce costs for firms, for instance enabling them to access several major conurbations from a single office, and it could provide access to more significant markets, including labour markets. This would be comparable with the situation in western Germany where the high speed line between Frankfurt and Cologne (roughly the same distance as between Birmingham and Leeds) is enabling workers to access job opportunities in both cities.

3.20 Over the longer term, it could have more profound effects, improving overall productivity and competitiveness in the Midlands and the North by encouraging greater specialisation in urban economies, building for instance on Leeds' growing reputation as a financial centre, and Manchester's strength in the creative and media industries over the past 50 years, which has been underlined by the BBC's recent decision to relocate a significant part of its activities to Salford Quays.

3.21 To support such a pattern of increasing specialisation and economic productivity, the Midlands and the Northern regions have significant resources upon which they can draw. They contain no fewer than seven universities in the Times World Top 100: Manchester, Warwick, Birmingham, York, Sheffield, Nottingham and Leeds; as well as major international airports at Manchester and Birmingham, strong regional airports at Leeds Bradford, Liverpool, and in the East Midlands; major port facilities, highly developed supply chains, important research and development facilities (such as Astra Zeneca's Cheshire plant), and long-standing traditions of excellence and innovation in advanced manufacturing and engineering.

3.22 Furthermore, released capacity on conventional rail networks could also help to support regional growth by enabling improved commuter services into major cities, and by allowing levels of rail freight into key interchanges in the Midlands and North West to increase substantially.

3.23 By transforming the connectivity of the Northern and Midlands regions to London they would also be better placed to attract firms and business areas which would otherwise be expected to be based close to the capital. Sir Rod Eddington's study of transport and productivity in the UK stressed the importance of 'there-and-back-in-a-day' travel between key economic centres, but further reductions in journey times enabling half-day business trips, such as those potentially delivered through high speed rail, could have a long-term impact on decisions such as business location.

High Speed Rail

3.24 Currently firms wishing to tap into the London market tend to congregate in areas within an hour to 80 minutes of London, along with the back office functions for some major London businesses. In part as a result of this, a correlation can be seen between the rail journey time from London of British towns and cities and the value of the goods and services they produce (known as Gross Value Added (GVA)), as Figure 3.2 shows.

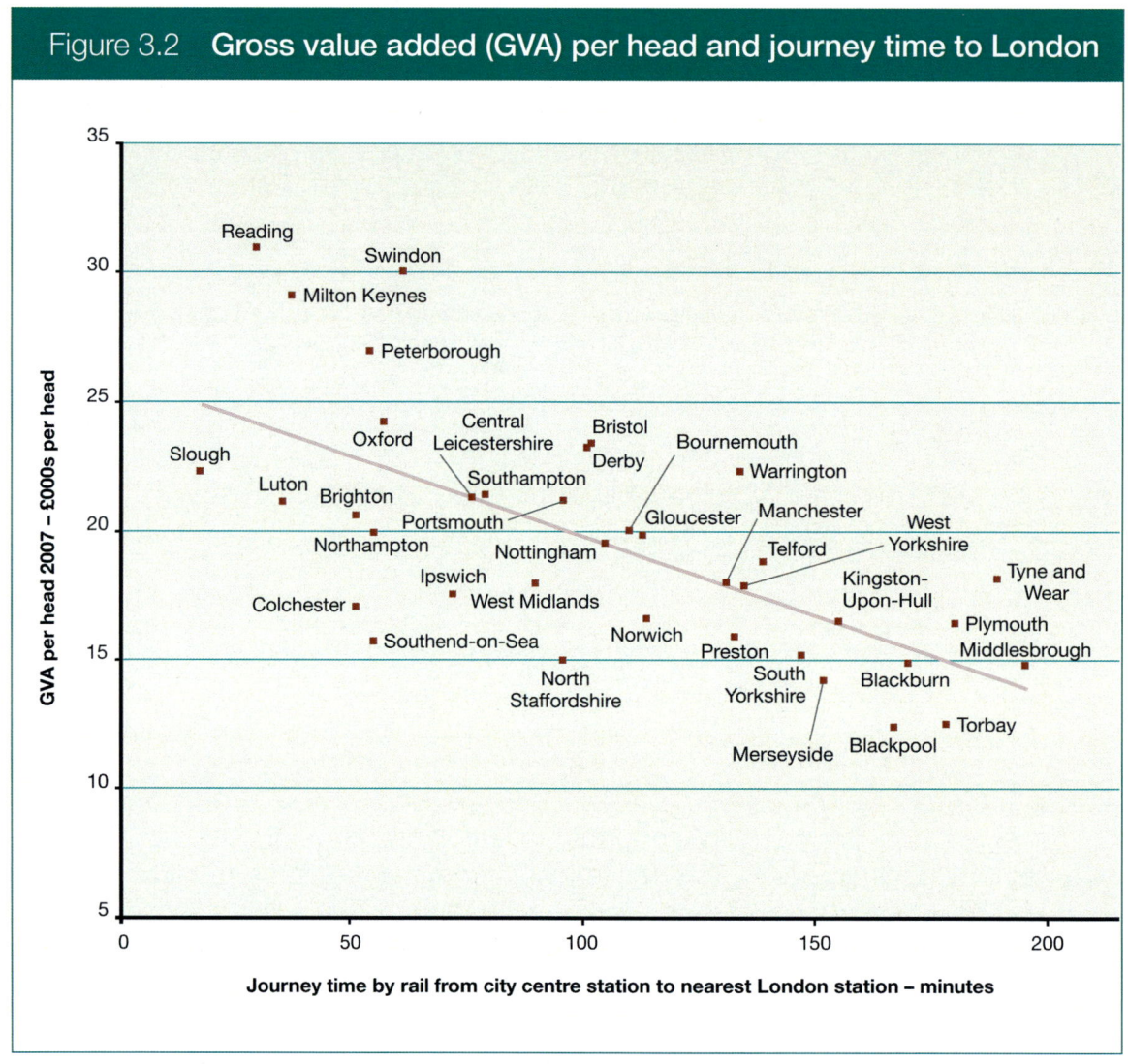

Figure 3.2 Gross value added (GVA) per head and journey time to London

3.25 Journey time from London is not the only factor taken into account in business location decisions, as evidenced by the significant differences in GVA between towns at roughly the same distance from the capital, such as Swindon and Southend. The availability of the right skills, together with issues such as cost, wider market access and quality of life, are other factors.

3.26 However, as noted above, the major cities of the Midlands and the North are home to major education and cultural sectors, and can offer a lower cost of living than London and the South East, and potential access to very significant regional markets. As such, bringing these cities closer to London, and reducing journey times to less than 80 minutes in all cases, and just 40-49 minutes for Birmingham, has significant potential to generate additional regional growth by influencing long term business location decisions.

Supporting housing growth

3.27 A British high speed rail network could also bring important housing benefits for the UK, in particular supporting housing growth in key towns and cities to the north of London.

3.28 The Government sees increasing the supply of housing as a key priority for tackling housing affordability and homelessness. The Milton Keynes/South Midlands sub-region (MKSM) has been identified as one of the major areas for that growth to take place, due to its potential for strong economic development and new housing development, and its proximity to both London and Birmingham.

3.29 Around 225,000 new homes and 200,000 new jobs are planned for the sub region over the next 10 years, with a further 100,000 new homes in the following decade. Whilst the region already has good links to London and Birmingham via the West Coast Main Line, improved transport provision has been identified as a key part of the MKSM delivery plan.

3.30 The improvements to journey times, capacity and reliability provided by the recent modernisation of the West Coast Main Line have already helped make the MKSM sub-region a more attractive proposition for business and for people commuting to London or Birmingham. But services to and from London remain highly congested at peak times, and this will worsen considerably over the coming 20 years without substantial increases in rail capacity.

3.31 HS2 Ltd's modelling of a London-Birmingham high speed line suggests that it could liberate sufficient capacity on the existing line to run a substantially improved service to Milton Keynes, Rugby and Northampton, potentially including seven non-stop services and five stopping services an hour from Milton Keynes to London at peak times.

3.32 The extension of High Speed Two to Leeds via the East Midlands and South Yorkshire would have the potential to deliver even greater benefits to key growth points within the MKSM sub-region, including Kettering, Wellingborough, Bedford and Luton, by removing many long distance services from the Midland Mainline and creating space for commuter capacity to grow as a result. Moreover, the released capacity delivered on the East Coast Main Line by a Leeds extension would help support housing growth in Peterborough, one of the key towns in the London-Stansted-Cambridge-Peterborough growth area.

3.33 In this way, all four of the priority areas for housing growth identified by the Government could benefit directly from its investment in high speed rail. Ashford and the Thames Gateway are already reaping the benefits of the recently introduced domestic services on the High Speed One line to the east of London and into Kent (see Figure 3.1). London-Cambridge-Stansted-Peterborough could benefit from released capacity on the East Coast Main Line. And MKSM could potentially see substantial capacity increases for commuter and regional services, as a result of capacity created on the upgraded West Coast Main Line by a new high speed line to Birmingham and further north.

Supporting London's long term competitiveness

3.34 For London, the potential benefits of high speed rail would also be considerable. The core 'Y' high speed rail network described in the following chapter could bring at least six of the major cities of the Midlands and the North to within 80 minutes of London, enhancing access to concentrations of innovation, knowledge and skills, for instance from the major universities and research facilities based in those city regions. By providing direct links to Crossrail, Heathrow and potentially High Speed One, the integration of the urban, national and international networks serving the capital could be significantly enhanced.

3.35 A new high speed rail network could bring other economic benefits for London. By basing the London terminus at a rebuilt Euston station, as HS2 Ltd have recommended, it could promote the further development of the Euston Road Corridor, alongside the new St Pancras terminus, as well as the British Library, the Wellcome Institute and the planned UK Centre for Medical Research and Innovation (see Sir Terry Farrell's commentary in Chapter 6). It could also contribute to the development of a key regeneration area in West London through the proposed Crossrail Interchange at Old Oak Common.

3.36 The Mayor of London states in his draft Economic Development Strategy that he *"supports the proposal of a north-south high speed rail line, which would help economic development and release some airport capacity."*[6]

The Government's conclusions

3.37 A high speed rail network connecting London with key city regions in the Midlands and the North, as well as offering through services to Scotland and the North East via existing lines, could offer significant wider economic benefits for the UK, over and above the conventional transport benefits which informed the conclusions set out in Chapter Two.

3.38 These could include agglomeration benefits for London and other major cities, enabling firms to access wider labour markets, and customer and supply bases. A high speed network could also promote more effective integration of city economies, permitting increasing specialisation and

---

[6] *The Mayor's Economic Development Strategy: Public Consultation Draft* (2009); at http://lda-consult.limehouse.co.uk/portal/eds/eds

productivity, and influencing national and international business location decisions.

3.39 A high speed network would also support the Government's housing growth objectives, as the capacity that it would release on existing rail lines would permit a significant increase in commuter and regional services to the key MKSM growth area. It could also support the long term competitiveness of the London economy, as well as the development of key regeneration areas in the capital.

3.40 These benefits are significantly more difficult to value than the conventional transport benefits used as the basis for the Government's appraisal in Chapter Two – although HS2 Ltd's assessment of the potential agglomeration and wider economic benefits of a London to Birmingham line indicates that they could be substantial.

3.41 Given their uncertainty, the Government has not included these benefits as part of its core assessment of the case for high speed rail in the UK. But it notes that they are potentially very significant, and that they would be in addition to the conventional transport benefits underpinning its conclusion that high speed rail offers unmatched potential for addressing the UK's long-term inter-city transport challenges.

3.42 The Government will carry out further work to assess the growth opportunities that high speed rail could deliver, in order that this might inform the future development of Regional Strategies and Local Development Frameworks where appropriate.

4. A Core High Speed Rail Network

Introduction

4.1 This chapter considers the possible scope of a British high speed rail network, drawing on HS2 Ltd's analysis of the options for linking London to Scotland. Its assessment is that the UK's initial core high speed rail network should consist of a Y-shaped set of routes connecting London to Birmingham, Manchester, the East Midlands, Sheffield and Leeds, with through services running onto the conventional network to additional destinations, including Liverpool, Newcastle, Glasgow and Edinburgh.

4.2 This network of around 335 miles, which would be capable of carrying trains at up to 250 miles per hour, would bring the West Midlands within about half an hour of London, and deliver journey times of 75 minutes from Leeds, Sheffield and Manchester to the capital. It would also transform connectivity between Birmingham and cities in the East Midlands, the North and Scotland, for instance halving the current journey times from Birmingham to Manchester and Leeds.

The economic geography of Britain

4.3 Britain's largest conurbations are tightly packed into a roughly triangular wedge heading from London to the North West and Yorkshire, as the population map of Britain at Figure 4.1 shows.

4.4 This area encompasses England's four most significant economic centres: London, Birmingham, Manchester and Leeds, and their surrounding areas, as well as Liverpool, Sheffield and the cities of the East Midlands. It also highlights, further north, the major cities of Scotland and the North East, and Bristol and the cities of South Wales to the west. But the most concentrated areas of economic activity can still be clearly discerned.

4.5 As the Eddington study notes, this means that the UK has different transport challenges from some of its major European competitors:

"the UK, like the Netherlands, has a high number of large settlements in close proximity to each other, whereas countries such as France and Spain may be characterised as having a greater dispersal of urban areas."

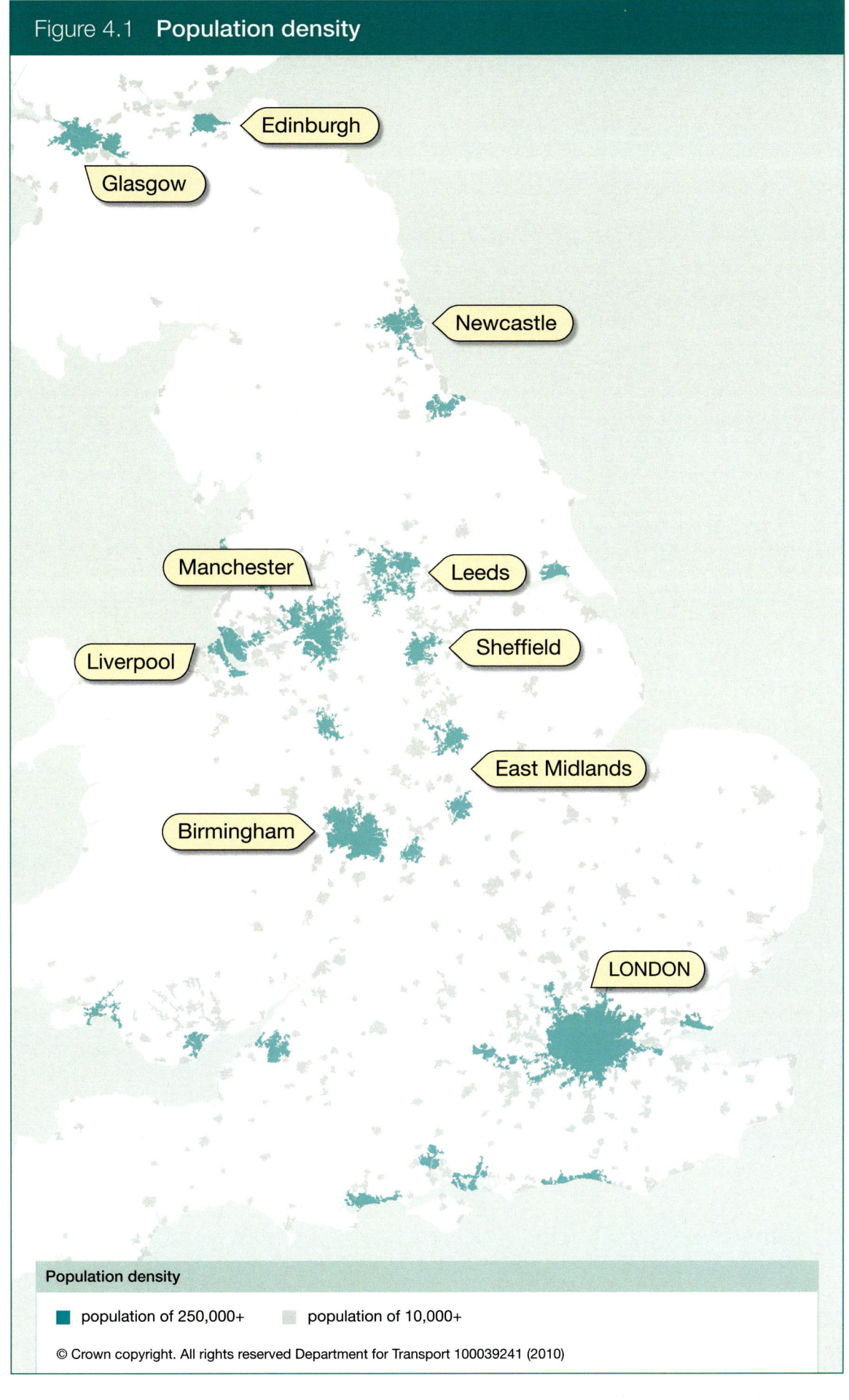

High Speed Rail

4.6 It has been argued that this tightly packed economic geography means that high speed rail is of less potential benefit to the UK than to other countries, as key urban centres are already generally within one day's return rail travel of one another. However, this contention is not borne out by experience elsewhere.

4.7 Many of the most successful high speed lines connect cities as close to or closer to one another than those in the UK. Within France, the first and most-heavily used TGV line connects Paris to Lyon, a distance of about 265 miles and comparable with the distance from London to Newcastle upon Tyne. The most heavily used section of the Japanese Shinkansen (indeed, the most heavily used high speed rail line in the world) is only just over 300 miles long, from Tokyo to Osaka. This line includes 14 intermediate stations, providing high speed connectivity for journeys of all distances.

4.8 Similarly, some of Germany's most successful high speed lines link cities no further apart than those in England. The only line in Germany which has been almost entirely upgraded to high speed is between Frankfurt and Cologne, a distance of around 110 miles – roughly the same as between London and Birmingham. The recently completed high speed line between Amsterdam and Brussels is just over 120 miles long and the distance from Paris to Le Mans on the French *LGV Atlantique* line is only slightly further.

4.9 All of these European lines link into their host country's conventional rail network, enabling services to continue at slower speed to more distant destinations. This principle should also underpin the British high speed network.

4.10 The UK's economic geography therefore makes it well suited to high speed rail. The capacity and connectivity between its largest conurbations could potentially be transformed by a relatively short network of high speed lines. As can be seen from the table below, the core network required to connect the UK's four largest cities would be shorter than for any comparable country other than Japan.[7]

Table 4.1	Current or projected national high speed rail networks	
Country	**Largest Cities**	**Approx Length of Track**
UK	London, Birmingham, Manchester, Leeds	335 miles
France	Paris, Lyon, Marseille, Lille/Roubaix	475 miles
Japan	Tokyo, Yokohama, Osaka, Nagoya	320 miles
Spain	Barcelona, Madrid, Seville, Valencia	890 miles
Germany	Berlin, Hamburg, Munich, Cologne	708 miles
Italy	Turin, Milan, Rome, Naples	545 miles

---

[7] The figures for the UK are derived from HS2 Ltd's calculations for their 'inverse A' network; figures for France, Japan, Spain and Italy are based on current and/or planned high speed rail networks; figures for Germany are a rough approximation based on driving distance.

A Core High Speed Rail Network

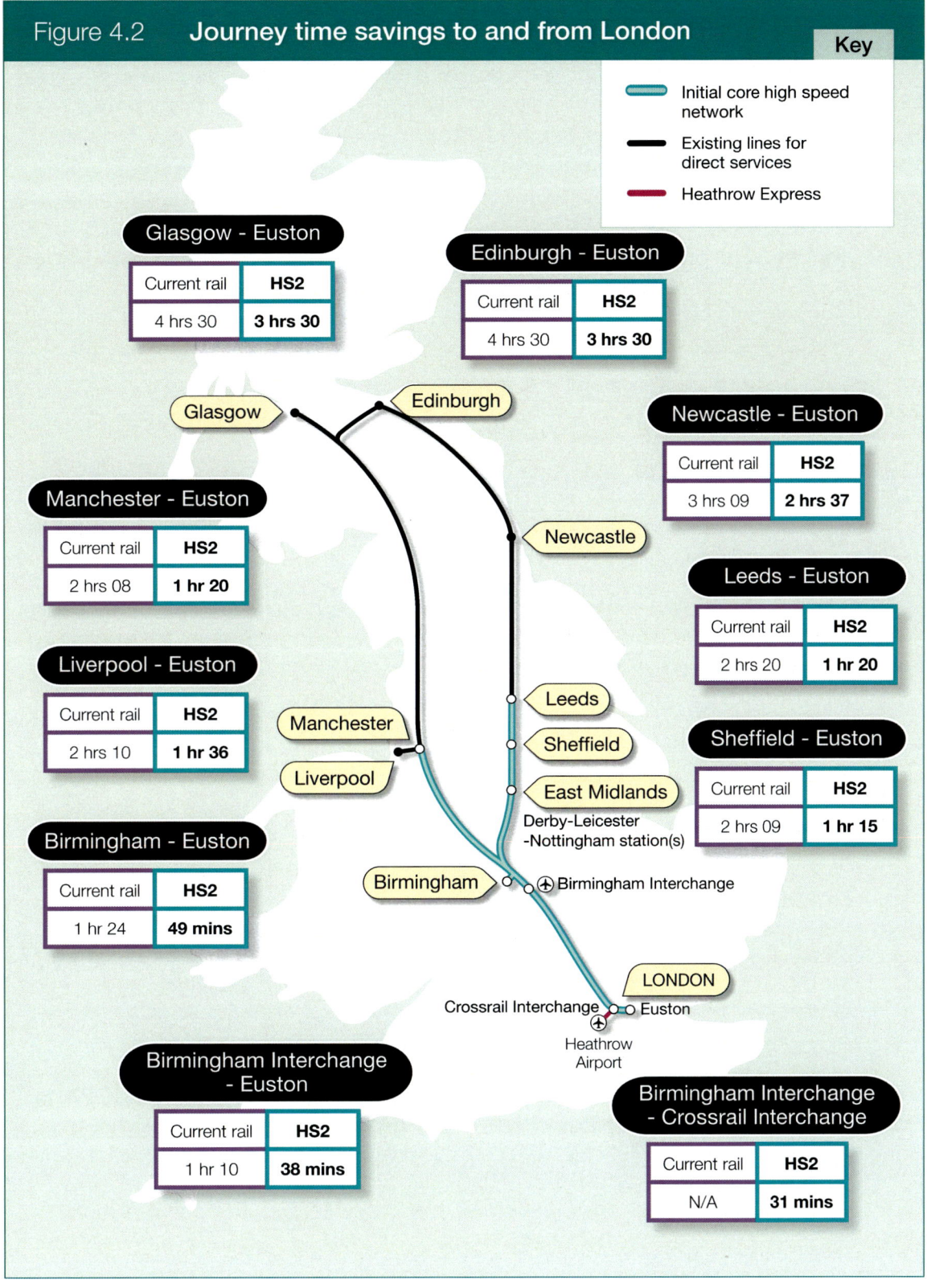

Figure 4.2 Journey time savings to and from London

4.12 It is therefore important in considering the case for high speed rail not just to look at a single route, but to analyse the options for a wider network in order to identify the proposal which would offer the greatest value for Britain at large. The Government believes that the core network should include direct links to the four largest English conurbations, as identified above. It should also make provision, from the outset, for through services to cities further north, before any decisions are taken about subsequent extensions of the high speed line to these destinations. This mirrors the successful experience of France, where TGV services have long run beyond the high speed network onto conventional lines to major cities including Bordeaux, Rennes and Nice, destinations to which the high speed lines are planned to be extended.

The case for the 'Y'

4.13 A high speed line from London to the West Midlands alone would deliver capacity increases and reduced journey times to cities in the North West and Scotland, by allowing long-distance services from London to continue at conventional speed onto the West Coast Main Line.

4.14 However, the Government's assessment is that such a short stretch of line on its own would not be the optimal way forward, other than as the first stage in the development of a more extensive high speed network. It has taken into account three key factors in reaching this view.

4.15 Firstly, the per mile costs of the London-Birmingham line would be substantially higher than of any extension north, as it would have to address the particularly expensive challenges of delivering a viable London terminus, a Crossrail Interchange, and a route out of the capital. Extensions of the line to major cities north of Birmingham would be likely to be achievable at a significantly lower per mile cost. HS2 Ltd estimate the infrastructure cost of linking England's four largest cities with a roughly 335-mile Y-shaped network would be around £30 billion, compared to between £15.8 and £17.4 billion for the first 128 miles of track from London to the West Midlands alone. Given that the extended 'Y' network would also greatly increase the benefits, this suggests that it would be likely to improve overall value for money.

4.16 Secondly, the journey time savings offered by a London to Birmingham line alone to destinations north of the West Midlands and, in particular, to Scotland are valuable, but not sufficient to deliver sizeable modal shift from air, with the journey times from Glasgow to London not dropping below four hours at best, which is barely faster than today's fastest train services.

4.17 Thirdly, the London to Birmingham route alone would not provide any opportunity for high speed services to connect with the East Coast or Midland Main Lines. Therefore it would not deliver any connectivity or capacity improvement for destinations to the east of the country, including Sheffield, Leeds and the cities of the East Midlands. Nor would it release any capacity for additional commuter services on the congested stretches of those lines close to London. By contrast, the 'Y' would offer transformational connectivity and capacity benefits from London to destinations on both the Midland and East Coast Main Lines, delivering a journey time from London to the East Midlands of as little as 50 minutes and to Leeds of around 75 minutes.

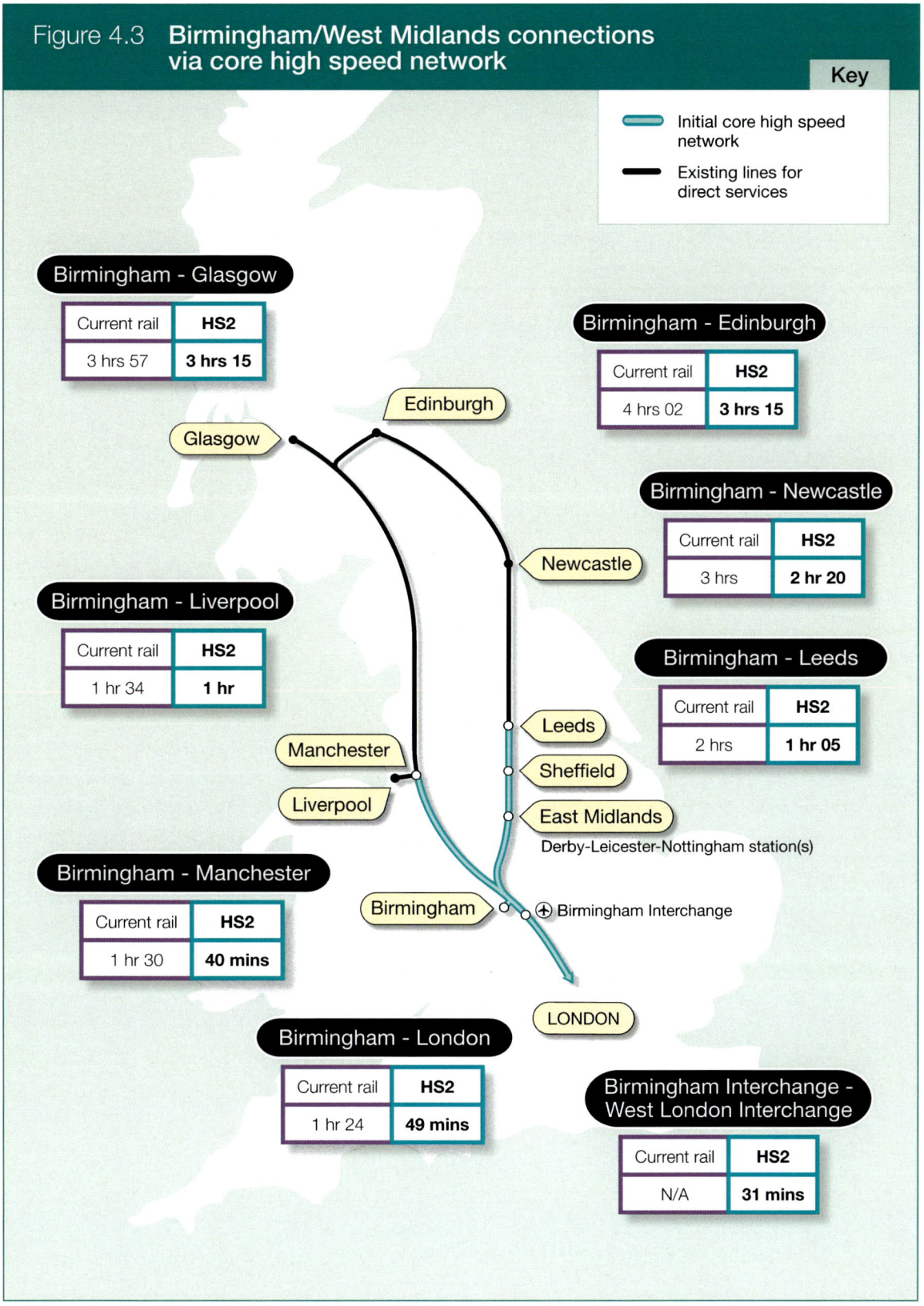

Figure 4.3 Birmingham/West Midlands connections via core high speed network

4.18 To appreciate the full and potentially transformational benefits of the 'Y' network, it is important to recognise the opportunity it provides to overcome the acute connectivity limitations of the Victorian rail network, whose three separate and poorly-inter-connected main lines from London to the North have survived largely unchanged to the present day, each with its own separate London terminus. Leeds would be less than 20 track miles further from London on the proposed 'Y' high speed network routed via Birmingham, yet such a high speed line would slash the journey time to the capital from both Leeds and Sheffield, whilst also halving journey times to Birmingham, whose connectivity with these Yorkshire cities is currently very poor (see paragraph 3.15).

4.19 Conceptually, the 'Y' network would unite the West Coast Main Line, the Midlands Main Line and the East Coast Main Line into a single, integrated high speed line for long-distance services into London, with a Birmingham Interchange station – on the eastern edge of the city, close to Solihull and Coventry – at the junction of the high speed routes north towards Manchester and beyond; and north east to the East Midlands, Sheffield, Leeds and beyond. Furthermore, the 'Y' network would overcome the historical route limitations of the West Coast Main Line itself, which reaches Birmingham via a long spur from Rugby, severely limiting connectivity between Birmingham and Manchester, Britain's second and third largest cities and economic centres. Figure 4.4 indicates these old and new network connections.

4.20 By including a Crossrail Interchange station as part of the core 'Y' network, all of these cities would gain further connectivity benefits, as this would deliver a fast and frequent service to London's West End, City and Docklands districts, providing a level of connectivity to all of the major economic, business and cultural centres of central and east London unmatched by any London terminal today.

4.21 This core high speed network, the 'Y', therefore offers a once-in-a-lifetime opportunity not only to accelerate train services between Britain's major conurbations, but also to reinvent the inter-city rail network itself. It could transform inter-urban connectivity as well as the speed of services, and overcome the severe limitations of the Victorian north-south network, built by separate competing companies, which has remained sacrosanct for too long.

A Core High Speed Rail Network

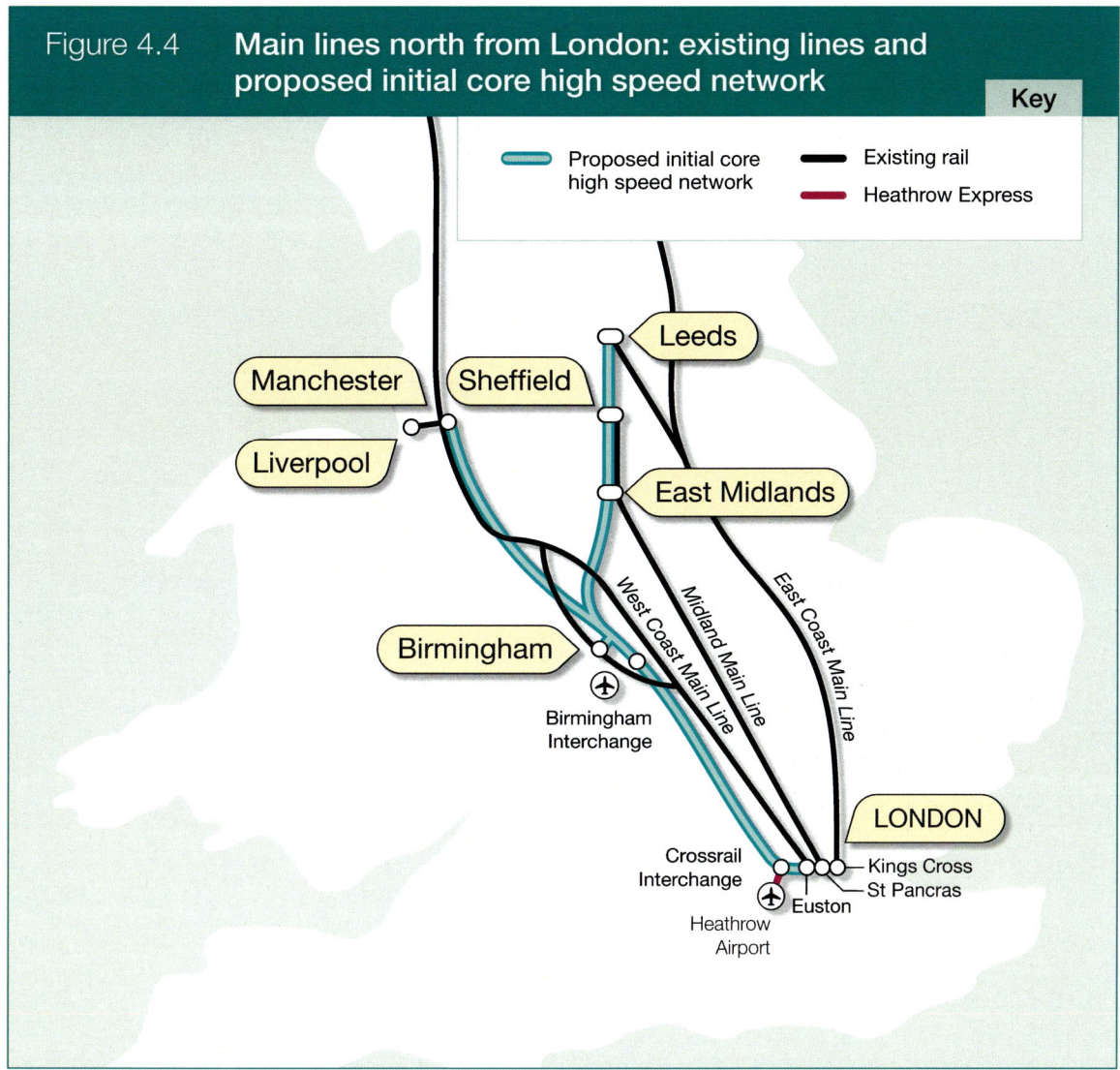

Figure 4.4 Main lines north from London: existing lines and proposed initial core high speed network

HS2 Ltd's analysis of options for a wider network

4.22 The Government's proposal for a Y-shaped network linking London to Birmingham, Manchester and Leeds has been informed by an analysis carried out by HS2 Ltd of the options for extending the high speed network north from Birmingham to Scotland.

4.23 HS2 Ltd considered three options for such a wider network, which are set out in Figure 4.5.

4.24 Of these options, HS2 Ltd's analysis suggests that although it is not the shortest or cheapest option, the 'Inverse A' is likely to present the best business case. This is because its additional costs are more than outweighed by the improved journey times it offers to the widest range of destinations, and the additional growth in the market, including as a result of modal shift from aviation, that it would attract as a result.

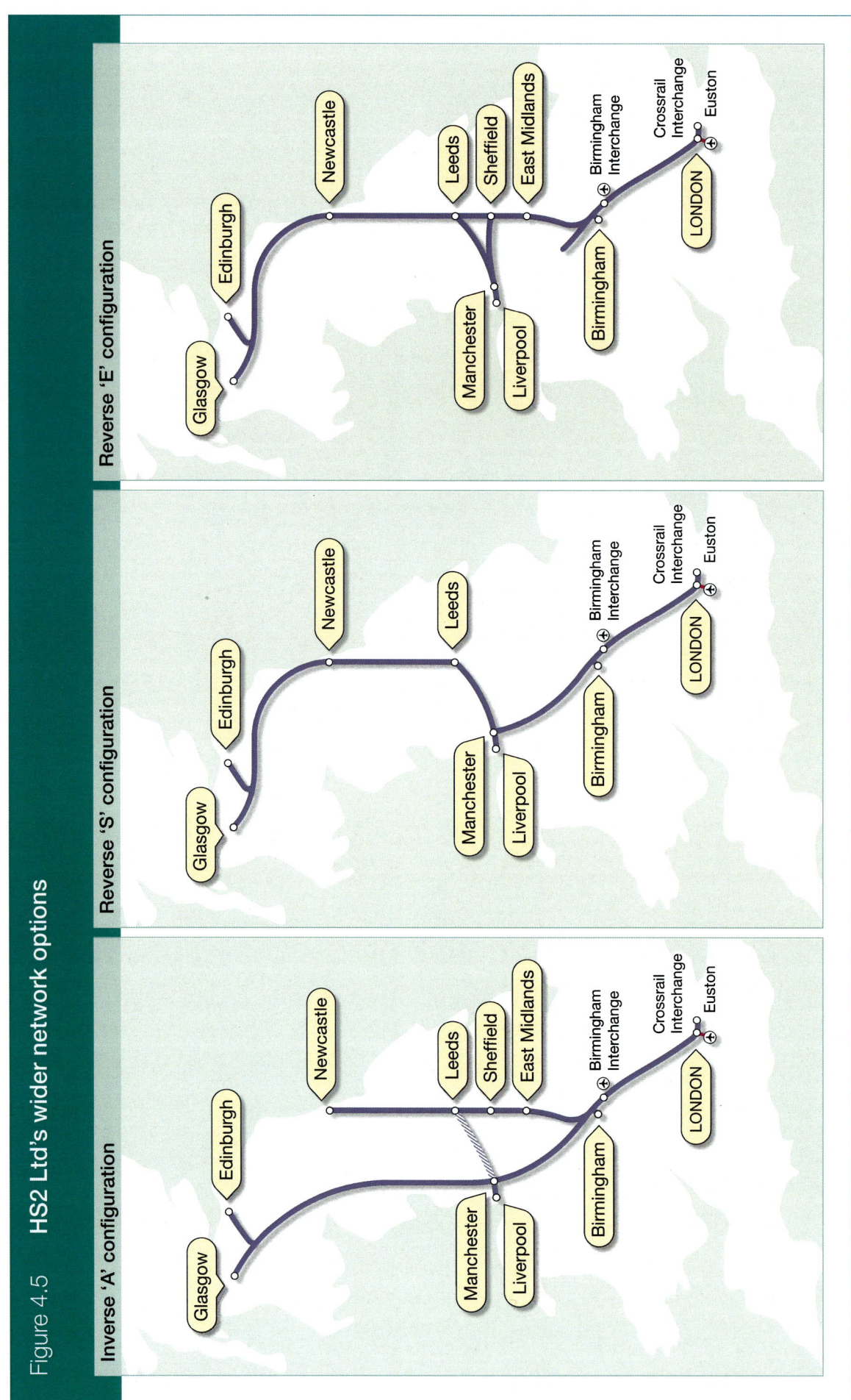

Figure 4.5　HS2 Ltd's wider network options

4.25 HS2 Ltd also noted that this 'Inverse A' network could be built in stages, beginning with the legs to Manchester and Leeds. Each of these two legs would be likely to have a strong business case as an addition to the initial London-Birmingham line, and their completion would deliver the core 'Y' network described above, as well as providing a foundation for any continuations north.

4.26 HS2 Ltd's analysis is summarised in Table 4.2 below.

Table 4.2 Comparison of HS2 Ltd's wider network options

Journey Times (hrs:mins)

Route	Inverse A	Reverse S	Reverse E
London-Manchester	1:20	1:20	1:40
London-Leeds	1:20	1:35	1:20
London-Newcastle	2:00	2:07	2:00
London-Glasgow/Edinburgh	2:40	3:17	3:10
Birmingham-Manchester	0:40	0:40	1:28
Birmingham-Leeds	1:05	1:07	1:05
Manchester-Glasgow/Edinburgh	1:45	2:48	3:15/3:30

Business Case

	Inverse A	Reverse S	Reverse E
Infrastructure Capital Cost	£52.2 bn	£44.3 bn	£49 bn
Benefits	£103 bn	£73.9 bn	£87.3bn
Indicative Benefit:Cost Ratio	2.3:1	1.8:1	1.9:1

4.27 In considering the journey times and benefit:cost ratios set out above, it should also be borne in mind that the journey times from Birmingham to Leeds and Newcastle for the 'Inverse A' and the 'Reverse E' include stops at additional stations in the East Midlands, South Yorkshire and Teesside, offering wider connectivity benefits that the 'Reverse S' cannot provide.

4.28 Although HS2 Ltd's work suggests that the 'Inverse A' is likely to be the best candidate, it does not offer a definitive view as to the precise configuration of the optimum wider network, given the strategic nature of its analysis. Rather, it limits itself to a small number of broader conclusions, which are set out below:

- *There is a good case for going on to develop high speed lines beyond the West Midlands and, of the networks we have looked at, a network with two branches either side of the Pennines performs best.*

- *While there appears to be a good case for continuing High Speed Two on to the North West and Manchester, there looks also to be a particularly strong case for a branch to Yorkshire and Leeds, via the East Midlands. Both appear to be strong candidates for more detailed work as part of the next stage of development.*

- *Government needs to decide its aspirations for the longer term network before plans for the next stage can be worked up in detail. We have been able to design High Speed Two in such a way that options for the future remain open, but this will not be the case for route sections beyond Birmingham.*

- *The longer term network should initially be built out from the High Speed Two trunk. If there is further demand in the longer term, a second leg could be provided from the East Midlands to London.*

The 'Y' – a core high speed rail network for the UK

4.29 The Government accepts HS2 Ltd's analysis, and agrees with its conclusion that there is a good case for the UK's core high speed rail network to include branches to either side of the Pennines, connecting to both Manchester and Leeds. Its analysis of HS2 Ltd's 'Inverse A' option has also led it to make three further proposals.

4.30 First, the Government's view is that the potential benefits from connections to Manchester and Leeds are sufficiently high, and the credibility of the project sufficiently strong, that these links should be planned as part of Britain's initial core high speed network, the 'Y', subject to effective route planning and public consultation, and to the confirmation of the provisional benefits and economic case for the Manchester and Leeds extensions.

4.31 Second, the Government believes that the link between Manchester and Leeds would be best enhanced through consideration of options for a conventional upgrade of the existing line rather than through a new high speed line, given the proposals for upgrading the line contained in Network Rail's Northern Hub plan.

4.32 Third, the Government believes it imperative that Scotland and Northern England should gain the benefits of high speed services from the outset of any network. Significant journey time savings and connectivity benefits would flow to Scotland and Northern England from the through high speed trains which are part of the Government's core proposition. The Government will work with the devolved administrations in Scotland and Wales to ensure that any future plans for high speed services or lines are coordinated with their own transport plans.

4.33 At around 335 miles, this Y-shaped network would be less than half the length of the 'Inverse A' and substantially lower in cost. HS2 Ltd's analysis suggests that the infrastructure cost would be around £30 billion, compared to around £52.2 billion for the full 'Inverse A', yet it would be likely to deliver the great majority of its benefits. It would directly link all of the UK's four largest conurbations, as well as enhancing connectivity to two more key city regions through possible stations in the East Midlands and Sheffield.

A Core High Speed Rail Network

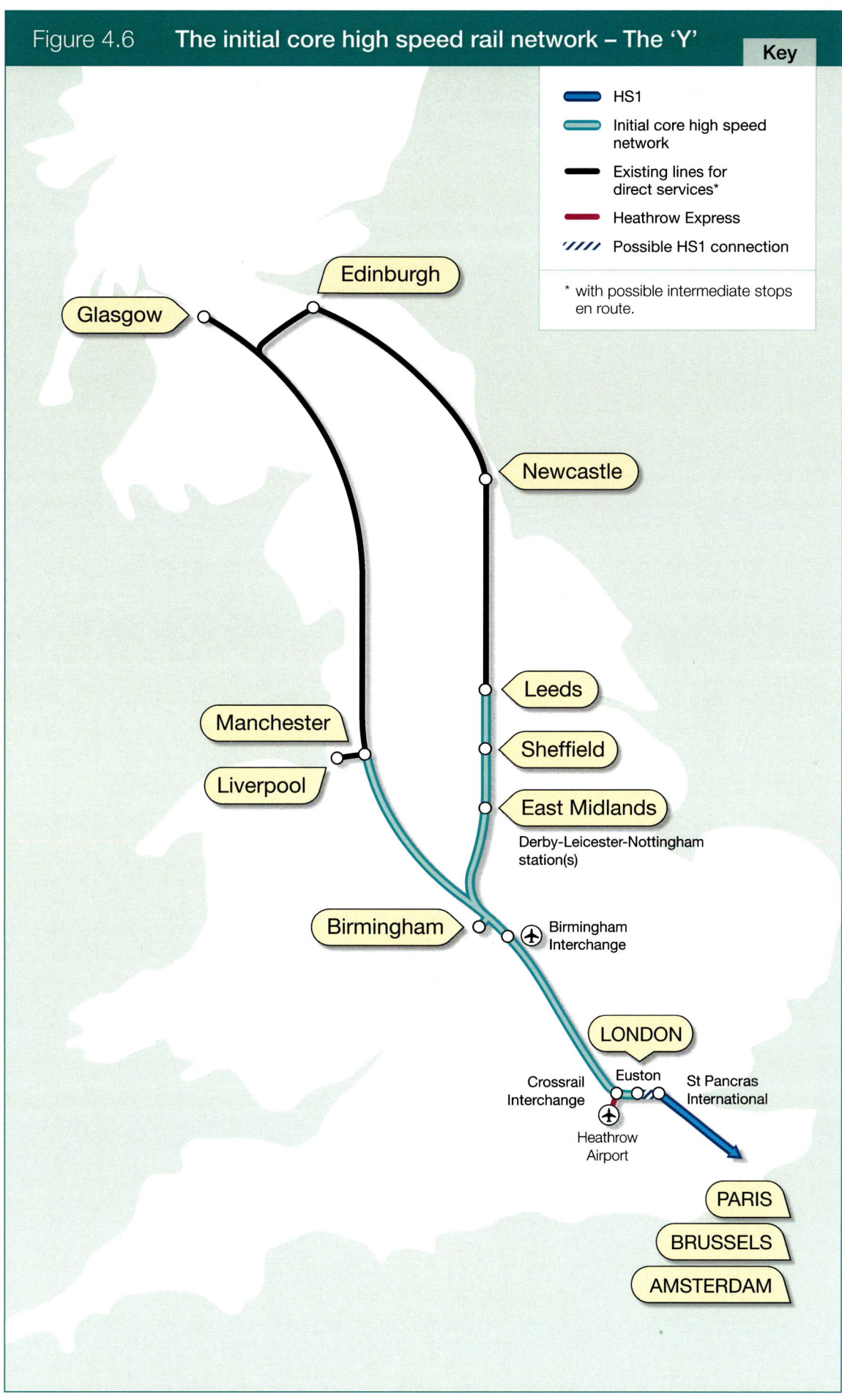

Figure 4.6 The initial core high speed rail network – The 'Y'

75

4.34 On the basis that it would be built to at least the same specification as the most recent TGV lines, allowing trains to run at up to 225 miles per hour, this 'Y' network would reduce the journey time from the centre of Birmingham to London to as little as 40-49 minutes, depending on the London station used, and would bring Manchester and Leeds within 40-45 minutes of Birmingham and 75 minutes of London.

4.35 Furthermore, a link into the East Coast Main Line at York would provide significantly improved journey times to Teesside, Newcastle and destinations further north by running onto the conventional network. And through a similar link onto the West Coast Main Line at Preston the journey time to Glasgow and Edinburgh could be cut to 3 hours 30 minutes, fast enough to generate the scope for significant modal shift from aviation.

4.36 HS2 Ltd's analysis suggests that by including links to Crossrail and the Heathrow Express in West London, end-to-end journey times to and from key business destinations could be reduced further still. Figure 4.7 sets this out in more detail.

4.37 The benefits of the 'Y' network would not be limited to those travelling to and from the destinations served. As set out in Chapter Two, by removing many long distance services from conventional lines, a high speed network can also release capacity for additional commuter and freight services. Unlike a London-Birmingham line, the 'Y' network would not only deliver such capacity increases on the West Coast Main Line. It would also see long-distance services reduced on the heavily used southern sections of the Midland and East Coast Main Lines, as long-distance services to the East Midlands, Sheffield and Leeds transferred to the new high speed lines.

4.38 These capacity increases would enable the numbers of commuter services to be expanded serving areas expected to see significant population growth, including the Milton Keynes/South Midlands Housing Growth Area, as well as other major towns and cities such as Luton and Peterborough.

4.39 The continuation of the 'Y' network beyond Birmingham to Manchester would also be likely to significantly improve its value in terms of increased freight capacity. HS2 Ltd's report notes that a high speed line to Birmingham alone would free up some additional freight paths on the southern stretch of the West Coast Main Line, but that the overall benefits would be limited by capacity constraints between Birmingham and the North West. Extending the network to Manchester would address these constraints and unlock a much more substantial increase in capacity on Britain's most heavily used rail freight artery. There would also be additional freight capacity on the East Coast Main Line and the Midland Main Line.

4.40 Developing the 'Y' high speed network would follow commitments from the Government's current rail investment plans which focus, following the completion of the West Coast Route Modernisation programme, on enhancing capacity on major commuter routes and on the electrification of the Great Western Main Line and key regional routes in the North West as the first part of a rolling programme of electrification.

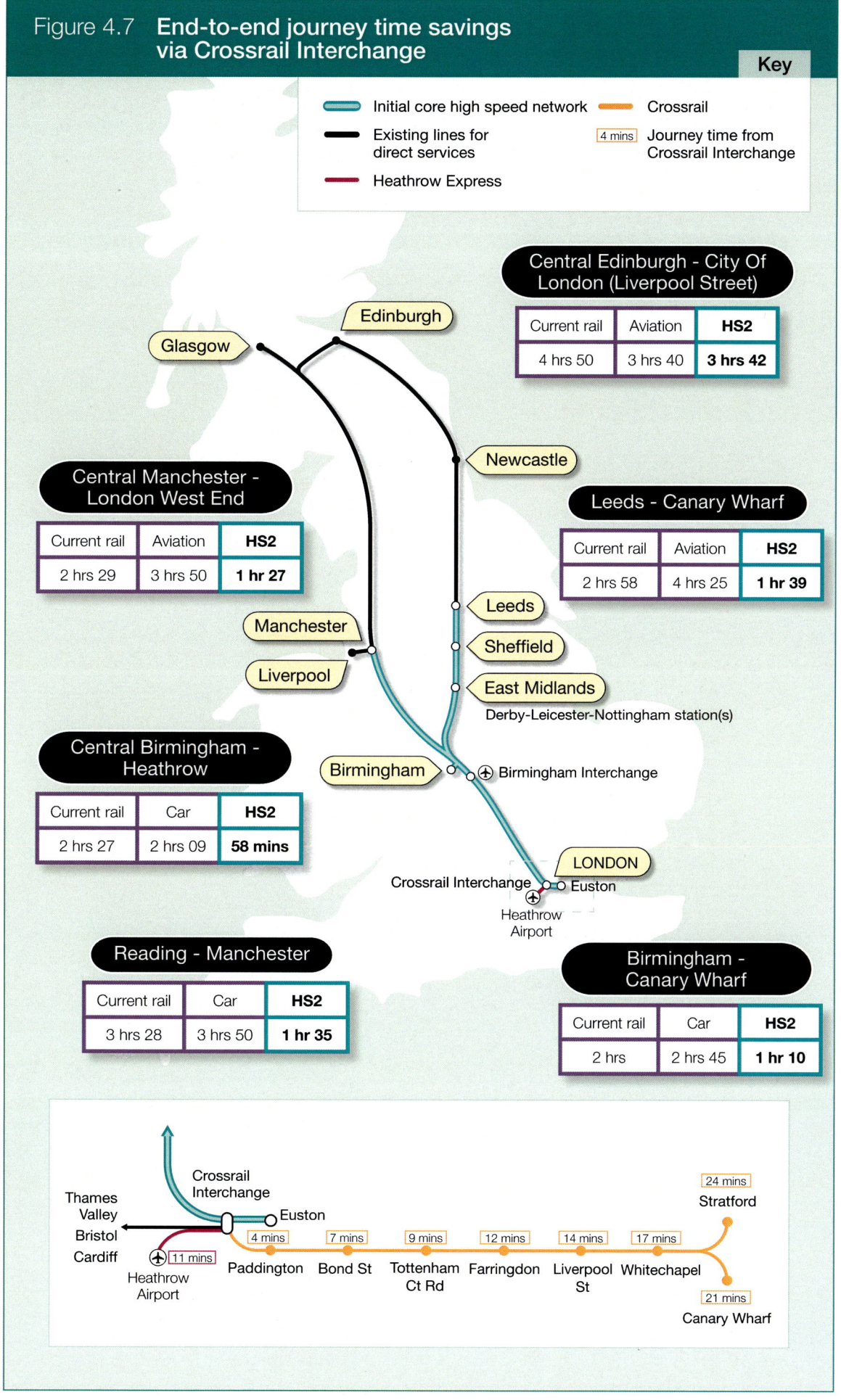

Figure 4.7 End-to-end journey time savings via Crossrail Interchange

4.41 It would also be consistent with a longer-term aspiration to see the network extended further to link directly to the cities of the North East and Scotland, and to other major destinations. If such extensions are to progress, it will be vital that the necessary planning work does not wait for the initial Y-shaped network to have been constructed.

4.42 However, the immediate priority for detailed route planning, in order to inform formal public consultation in due course, is to identify viable route options north from Birmingham to Manchester and Leeds.

The Government's proposed policy for a high speed network

4.43 The Government's first proposal is that the UK's initial core high speed network (the 'Y') should be planned to link London to Birmingham, Manchester, the East Midlands, Sheffield and Leeds.

4.44 The Government's second proposal is that this network should include connections onto existing tracks, including the West and East Coast Main Lines, so that direct high speed services can be operated from the outset to other cities including Glasgow, Edinburgh, Newcastle and Liverpool; and that consideration should be given to extending the network subsequently to these and other major destinations to further improve capacity and connectivity.

4.45 The Government's third proposal is that the capacity released through transferring long-distance services to this network should be used to expand commuter, regional and freight services on existing lines, with particular benefit for areas expected to see significant housing growth including Milton Keynes, Luton, Northampton, Peterborough, Kettering, Corby and Wellingborough.

4.46 Further work is now needed on the detailed route options to Manchester and Leeds and to assess fully their business cases. Formal public consultations will be held in due course on the Government's policy for high speed rail and on each element of the proposed network.

Part 2: High Speed Two – London to Birmingham

Euston Station, which opened in the 1830s, was extensively rebuilt during the 1960s. It continues to operate as the southern terminus of the West Coast Main Line, serving destinations in the West Midlands, North West and Scotland. Euston is proposed as the terminus for the new high speed line, and would be rebuilt, expanded and modernised to cater for existing and new traffic.

5. London to Birmingham

5.1 Part One of this Command Paper assesses the strategic case for high speed rail in the UK. It concludes that high speed rail offers benefits unmatched by any other major new infrastructure option for tackling the UK's inter-urban transport challenges over the next 20 to 30 years, and that an initial core high speed network linking London to Birmingham, Manchester and Leeds should be taken forward to public consultation.

5.2 However, it is one thing to make a strategic argument for high speed rail, and another to demonstrate that a British high speed line would be a credible and buildable project, especially given the challenges posed in identifying and constructing a London terminus and a route out of the city.

5.3 For this reason, HS2 Ltd was commissioned to develop a detailed proposal for a high speed line from London to Birmingham including potential route options, train service patterns, and costs for the development, construction and operation of the line.

5.4 London to Birmingham would be the essential first stage of any British high speed rail network for three reasons. First, the transport corridors north from London will be amongst the UK's most congested over the coming decades (as can be seen from the congestion maps reproduced in Chapter One). In conjunction with extensions to Manchester and Leeds, a London-Birmingham high speed line would relieve all three main rail lines and the major motorways serving these routes. Second, such a line would link – and transform connectivity between – the UK's two largest population and economic centres. And third, it would provide the necessary foundation to serve destinations further north and through to Scotland from the outset.

5.5 This Chapter describes the approach taken by HS2 Ltd in developing its recommendations and the basis on which the Government has assessed them. It then sets out the high-level results of that process, concluding that the business case for a London to Birmingham line is sound and that such a line is a viable project offering high value for money, with more than £2 of benefits for every £1 spent.

5.6 The following chapters consider each part of HS2 Ltd's proposed line in turn and set out the Government's response in each case, including the further work that it has commissioned where necessary.

The approach taken by HS2 Ltd

5.7 As a foundation for its detailed design and planning work, HS2 Ltd identified six key principles which underpin its recommendations for high speed rail in the UK. These principles are set out below:

   i. High speed capacity should be used in a way which yields the maximum overall benefit, given its high cost and expected strong demand.

   ii. High speed rail services should serve long distance, city-to-city journeys rather than shorter distance trips.

   iii. New high speed lines should only be used by high speed trains. Adding slower trains reduces capacity.

   iv. In the early stages of developing a network, the benefits should be extended to cities further north with trains running off the high speed line and onto the existing classic network. This is crucial to the business case.

   v. Over time, however, the longer term high speed network should become more segregated from the constrained classic network to maximise the benefits of reliability and capacity.

   vi. High speed lines must be well integrated with other transport networks to allow the time savings to be carried through to the whole end-to-end journey.

5.8 Building on these principles, HS2 Ltd's work was carried forward through a process of option sifting and assessment to identify the route and station choices which offered the highest value for money. This process included assessments of engineering and operational viability, financial cost, impact on journey times and capacity, and implications for the local environment and communities.

5.9 The assessment process was also underpinned by a project specification, which comprised the line's main technical, operational and environmental requirements and was drawn together on the basis of European and international best practice. The key principles of this project specification are summarised in the box overleaf.

5.10 Underlying HS2 Ltd's approach was also the requirement to achieve value for money, by striking an appropriate balance between costs and the design aims.

5.11 The service specification used to model the benefits of High Speed Two was based on the current maximum train speed on European high speed networks of around 360 kilometres per hour. This provides a realistic assessment of likely network performance, but does not rule out the option of introducing faster services as and when the technology develops to deliver these.

> **High Speed Two – Summary of Project Specification**
>
> a) The infrastructure is designed for speeds up to 400 kilometres per hour (roughly 250 miles per hour) – a higher maximum speed than existing lines but in line with designs for future routes in Europe.
>
> b) The adoption of proven European standards, technology and practice.
>
> c) 400m-long European-sized trains, which are higher and wider than UK rolling stock and with a capacity of up to 1100 seats.
>
> d) An initial capacity of up to 14 trains per hour for High Speed Two, rising ultimately to 18 with a longer term network and likely future technological development.
>
> e) A maximum train speed of 360 kph (225mph) is assumed at opening.
>
> f) The design should follow the Government's sustainable development objectives, avoiding as far as possible harm to the natural and built environment and to communities.

5.12 In developing its proposals, HS2 Ltd's approach involved discussions with more than 200 stakeholders and drew on both major project experience accumulated in the UK and overseas experience of high speed rail. Its robustness was tested through independent expert challenge and close collaboration with relevant organisations.

High Speed Two – the Government's assessment

5.13 The Government's key objectives for inter-urban transport are capacity, connectivity and sustainability, and it is on this basis that it has assessed HS2 Ltd's recommendations for a London-Birmingham line ("High Speed Two").

5.14 The assessment has focused in part on whether the potential capacity and connectivity benefits of High Speed Two would justify the substantial costs of such a line.

5.15 The assessment has also looked at the environmental impacts of HS2 Ltd's proposals. This includes the potential effect on overall greenhouse gas emissions, and particularly the local environmental impacts of the detailed route options. The Government has sought to identify for further consideration those options which are most consistent with its objectives for sustainable development. In some areas it has commissioned further work on mitigating negative impacts to ensure that those objectives can be met.

5.16 In making its overall assessment, the Government has taken into account not only the evidence on capacity, connectivity and sustainability presented by HS2 Ltd, but also its own analysis of the wider benefits that such a line might bring to the UK, including, for instance, the types of impacts on regional growth described in Chapter Three and its view of the potential long-term case for improved integration of urban, national and international networks.

5.17 The remainder of this chapter sets out HS2 Ltd's high-level findings, including their recommended route for a London-Birmingham line and their assessment of its costs and benefits, together with the Government's response to those findings.

High Speed Two – the recommended route from London to the West Midlands

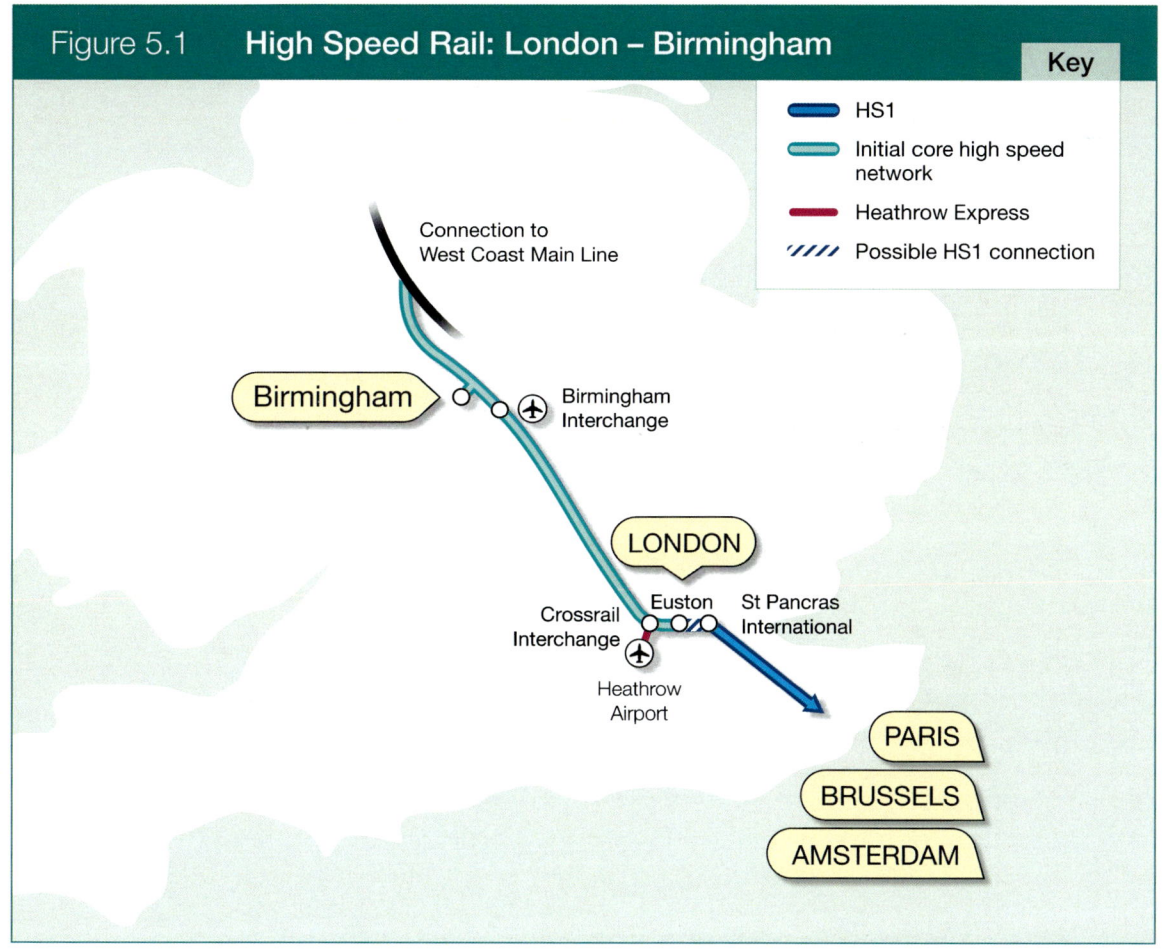

Figure 5.1 High Speed Rail: London – Birmingham

5.18 HS2 Ltd's recommended route for its proposed High Speed Two line would begin at a rebuilt and expanded Euston Station, and proceed in tunnel beneath north west London to surface at a new Crossrail Interchange station located at Old Oak Common (an existing railway facility in West London close to Willesden Junction). This would provide travellers with direct connections to Crossrail, Heathrow Express and the Great Western Mainline, helping to ease crowding at Euston and significantly improving links to such important business destinations as Canary Wharf, Heathrow Airport, the Reading/M4 corridor, and the City of London.

5.19 After departing from the Crossrail Interchange station, HS2 Ltd's recommended route would leave London via the Ruislip area, making use of an existing rail corridor. It would then cross the Chilterns in the Aylesbury direction, partly in tunnel before following the route of the A413 past Wendover. HS2 Ltd's report presents a number of options for this part of the journey, each of which presents different engineering and sustainability challenges with associated costs. These are considered in detail in Chapter Six.

5.20 North of the Chilterns, the recommended route would follow in part the disused Great Central rail alignment before passing Brackley and entering Warwickshire. It would then skirt to the east of Birmingham, to enter the city via a short link beginning in the Water Orton area, with the main line extending north to join the West Coast Main Line near Lichfield, enabling services to continue to Manchester, Liverpool and Glasgow on the conventional network.

5.21 A new Birmingham city centre station is recommended at Curzon/Fazeley Street, in the Eastside regeneration area, which would be developed to provide rapid and convenient access to the existing Moor Street and New Street stations.

5.22 A West Midlands interchange station is also recommended to be built to the south of Birmingham, extending the overall West Midlands market, and providing connections to Birmingham International Airport, the National Exhibition Centre and the motorway network. HS2 Ltd does not propose any other stations on route, arguing that intermediate destinations such as Milton Keynes would be better served through increases in commuter services made possible as a result of released capacity on existing lines.

5.23 Figure 5.2 provides a summary of HS2 Ltd's recommended scheme.

High Speed Two – the benefits

Capacity

5.24 In terms of capacity, HS2 Ltd's design would permit up to 14 train services an hour, rising to 18 an hour in future, subject to development of a more extended network and to future development of rolling stock and signalling technology.

5.25 The high speed trains would be formed of 200 metre sets, in line with European practice, and would carry up to 550 passengers (around 100 more than the current 9-car Pendolinos in use on the West Coast Main Line). For the services running entirely on high speed lines, it would be possible to operate two sets in formation, extending the length to 400 metres and increasing capacity to up to 1100 passengers.

5.26 Whilst decisions on actual service patterns would not be taken until a later stage, HS2 Ltd developed an initial service specification for modelling purposes to inform its assessment of the project's business case.

London to Birmingham

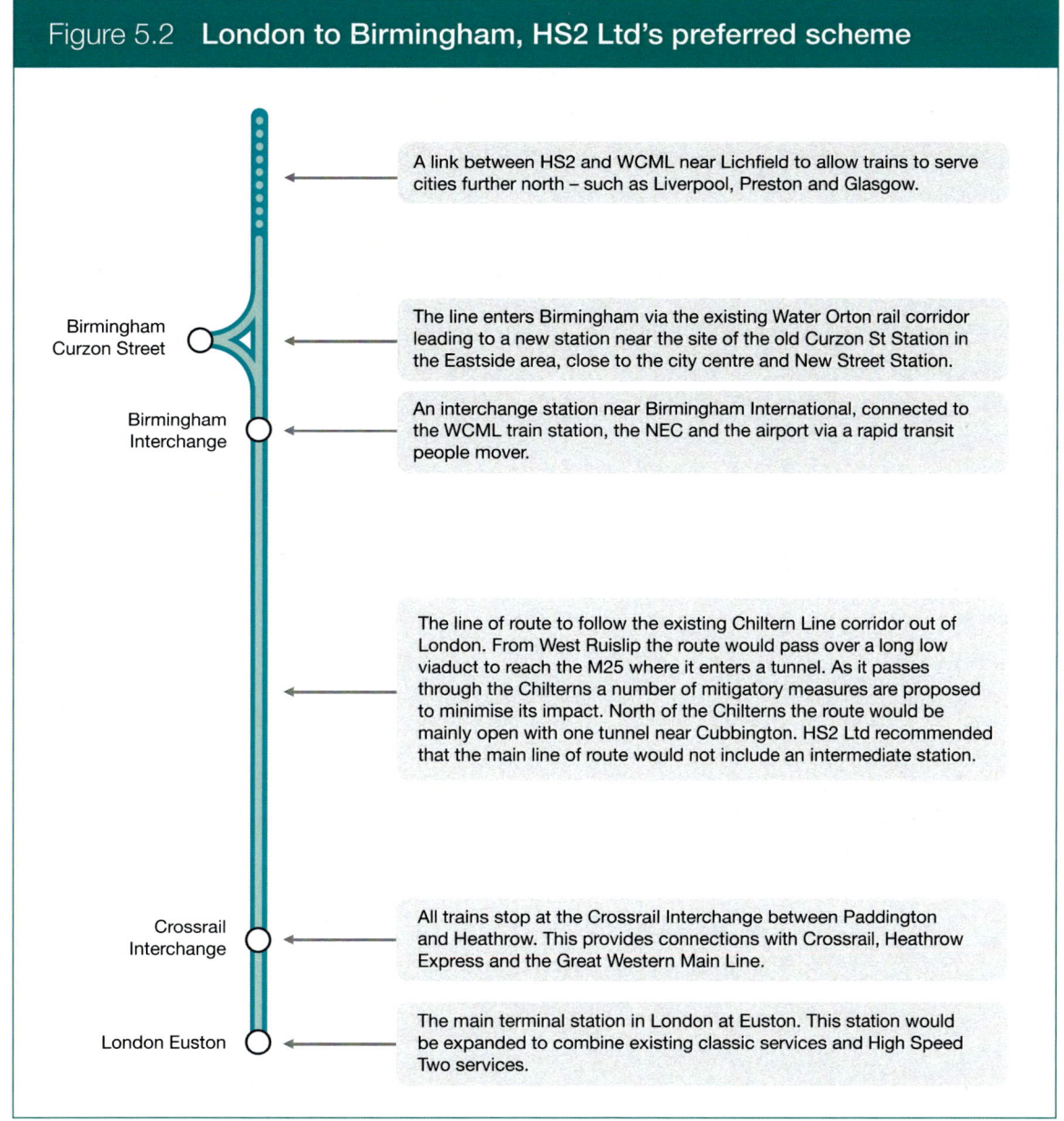

Figure 5.2 London to Birmingham, HS2 Ltd's preferred scheme

This made use of 11 train paths in the peak, on the basis that initial demand would not require every path to be used, and that additional services could be provided as demand increased over time.

5.27 As set out in Chapter Two, these long distance services would not be the sum total of the capacity benefits of High Speed Two. HS2 Ltd's modelling suggests that with the new high speed line in place there would be a reduction in the number of long distance passenger journeys made each day on the current West Coast Main Line from 105,000 to 20,000, allowing the removal of a large number of services to Birmingham, Manchester and other destinations which would be better served by the new line.

Figure 5.3 HS2 Ltd's preferred line of route – southern section

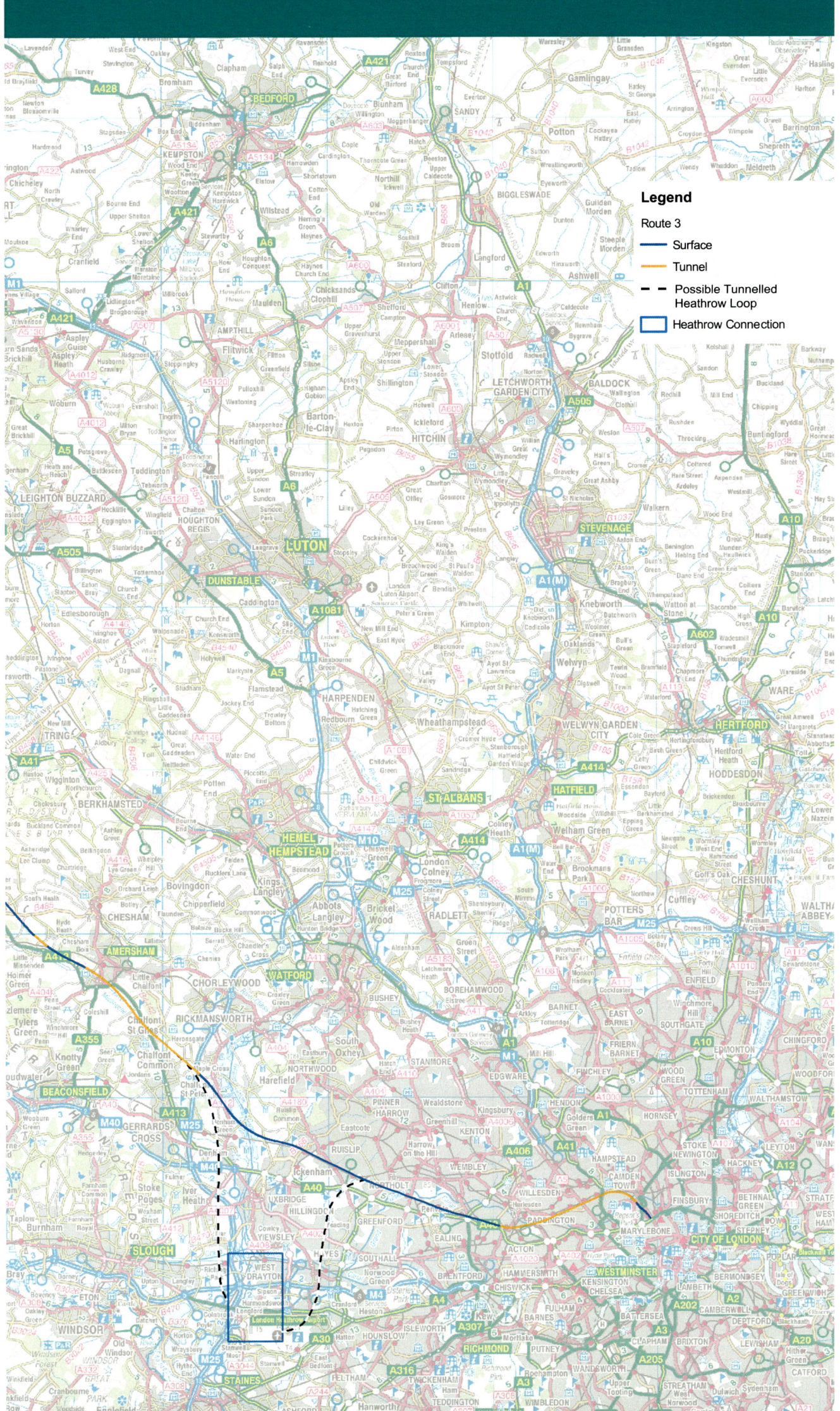

Figure 5.4 **HS2 Ltd's preferred line of route – northern section**

5.28 The removal of these services would release capacity on that route for additional commuter services to London and Birmingham, whilst still catering for rail freight growth and preserving long-distance services to other important destinations such as Crewe, Stoke-on-Trent, Wolverhampton and North Wales.

5.29 As a result of the released capacity it would be possible to run a substantially improved service to Milton Keynes, Rugby and Northampton, potentially including seven non-stop services an hour from Milton Keynes to London in the peak and five stopping services. This could help to address the significant increase in commuter demand expected as a result of the large amount of new housing planned in the Milton Keynes/South Midlands growth area.

5.30 Taken together, HS2 Ltd estimate that new infrastructure, longer trains and released capacity on the current network would see maximum potential capacity between London and the West Midlands increase by more than 200 per cent.

5.31 The Government's view is that these estimates of the capacity increases provided by High Speed Two are robust.

Connectivity

5.32 As well as this increase in rail capacity, High Speed Two would also significantly improve connectivity between London and Birmingham, as well as to a number of cities further north.

5.33 The journey time from London Euston to the centre of Birmingham would be reduced to just 49 minutes (an improvement of over half an hour from the current 1 hour 24 minute service). And the shortest West Midlands-London journey, from an interchange station close to Birmingham Airport to the Crossrail Interchange west of Paddington, would be quicker still, taking just 31 minutes.

5.34 The direct connections to Crossrail and the Heathrow Express provided by the Crossrail Interchange would cut journey times to key business destinations even further. The time taken to travel from central Birmingham to Canary Wharf would be halved from two hours to one by using the interchange station to connect to Crossrail, as opposed to using the current route from Euston via the Victoria and Jubilee Lines. The journey from central Birmingham to Heathrow via the Crossrail Interchange would be cut to under an hour, as opposed to the current two and a half hours by rail, or two hours by car. The proposed Birmingham Interchange station would reduce journey times from London to Birmingham Airport from 70 minutes to around 40 minutes.

5.35 These connectivity benefits would not be restricted to London and the West Midlands. The connection to the West Coast Main Line north of Birmingham would allow high speed trains to continue on the conventional network to major destinations further north, including Manchester, Liverpool and

Glasgow. In each case, these destinations would benefit from around a 30 minute saving on current average journey times.

5.36 The Government's view is that HS2 Ltd's assessment of the proposed line's connectivity benefits is robust.

Demand growth and modal shift

5.37 The UK is likely to see very significant growth in rail demand over the next 20 to 30 years, and will therefore need additional capacity to accommodate it. The substantial increases described above as a result of High Speed Two would allow the rail network to accommodate the forecast growth in demand for inter-urban travel over the coming decades, whilst still reducing crowding and incentivising travellers to shift from other modes due to improved connectivity.

5.38 The modelling carried out by HS2 Ltd estimates that without a new high speed line the current 45,000 long-distance journeys taken each day on the London to the West Midlands section of the West Coast Main Line will more than double by 2033 to around 105,000.

5.39 The consequence of this growth will be crowded trains throughout the day and severe congestion experienced routinely during peak hours. Even with lengthened trains and other planned improvements, the West Coast Main Line will effectively be full, with many potential travellers either discouraged from travelling altogether or forced to use other, more polluting modes such as aviation.

5.40 The picture would be very different with High Speed Two in place. In this case, HS2 Ltd's modelling suggests that the improvements in travel time and experience brought by the new line would attract a large number of additional travellers, with as many as 165,000 long-distance journeys being made on the same stretch of line in 2033, an increase of more than half on the base case.

5.41 Even allowing for this growth in traffic, the additional capacity provided by High Speed Two would significantly alleviate overcrowding for passengers. HS2 Ltd's modelling suggests that long distance services on the new line would have an average daily load factor of around 60 per cent, broadly in line with existing services but well below that which would be experienced if they continued to share space on existing lines with commuter, regional and freight services. Furthermore, substantially more commuter services could be run as a result of the reduction in long distance traffic on the West Coast Main Line, reducing crowding for passengers from Milton Keynes, Northampton and other towns on this route.

5.42 This is because, of the 105,000 long-distance passenger journeys predicted in 2033 without a new line, HS2 Ltd's modelling predicts that around 85,000 would switch to High Speed Two, with about 20,000 continuing to use the current network (to travel to intermediate destinations not served by high speed trains). Each of those passengers switching to the new line would benefit from the travel time savings they gain as a result, which would enable them to spend less time in transit and more time engaged in more productive or enjoyable activities.

5.43 This switch would not account for all of those who would be expected to use the new line. HS2 Ltd's modelling indicates that around 57 per cent of passenger journeys made on the new high speed journeys would otherwise have been made by conventional rail. A further 27 per cent would be entirely new journeys, made as a result of the enhanced connectivity offered by High Speed Two, and the final 16 per cent would have switched from other modes (roughly half from aviation and half from car).

5.44 The Government has reviewed this assessment of the additional demand and modal shift generated by High Speed Two, as well as the accompanying sensitivity analysis conducted by HS2 Ltd, and considers it a robust basis on which to calculate the benefits that the new line would provide.

Sustainability

5.45 Chapter 2 assessed the sustainability of high speed rail against other options for meeting the country's long term capacity and connectivity needs – and in particular its impact on overall carbon emissions in comparison with other modes. That assessment was based on HS2 Ltd's calculations of the carbon impacts of High Speed Two.

5.46 Its conclusion was that high speed rail would be relatively carbon efficient in comparison with most other ways of meeting the UK's inter-urban transport challenges over the next 20 to 30 years. It also concluded that the carbon impacts of High Speed Two, which HS2 Ltd calculated as being in a range from -25.0 million to +26.6 million tonnes over 60 years, could be accommodated within the Government's overall strategy for achieving its statutory target for reducing greenhouse gas emissions.

5.47 HS2 Ltd's design work also took into account the need for High Speed Two to be resilient to the unavoidable impacts of climate change.

5.48 The other sustainability impacts of any high speed rail project would depend very much on the specific route taken and mitigations put in place. To give just one example, impacts on landscape can be reduced through careful design (including following existing transport corridors) and use of tunnelling in the most sensitive areas.

5.49 HS2 Ltd carried out a careful analysis of the wider environmental and sustainability impacts of its recommended route, as well as substantial work on the options for mitigating these. HS2 Ltd's key conclusions are summarised below:

- Noise: About 350 dwellings could experience high noise levels, with a much larger number experiencing a noticeable noise increase. With additional mitigation these numbers could potentially reduce by half or more. The Government has commissioned HS2 Ltd to carry out further analysis to identify more precise noise impacts for settlements on the recommended route, and to consider the options for mitigating these through measures such as noise barriers or landscaping, prior to the commencement of any formal public consultation.

- Air Quality: The use of electric traction for rolling stock would mean that the operation of the High Speed Two would not itself have any air quality impacts. Some deterioration in air quality could be seen around stations if these attract significant car traffic, but this could be largely mitigated by ensuring good public transport links are in place.

- Landscape and townscape: Considerable work has already been undertaken to identify ways to mitigate landscape impacts, including using tunnelling and following existing transport corridors. There would be comparatively few impacts on townscape, but the works required to expand Euston station would require the removal of five blocks containing around 220 residential flats largely owned by Camden Council and a small number of other buildings. There would also be a number of properties elsewhere on the route which would need to be demolished.

- Heritage: The recommended route has been carefully designed to minimise heritage impacts, although a number of protected buildings and grounds would still be affected by it. In particular, the redevelopment at Euston would affect up to six Grade II listed structures, and the line of route recommended by HS2 Ltd would pass near a small number of protected buildings.

- Wildlife and biodiversity: The recommended route would avoid most potential impacts on designated habitats and sites. No international sites would be affected and impacts on nationally protected sites would be restricted to a few locations.

- Soil and land resources: High Speed Two would have a positive impact on the development of brownfield sites at Euston and Old Oak Common, and in Birmingham's Eastside regeneration area. Whilst HS2 Ltd's recommended route affects none of the most productive Grade 1 farmland, it does cross some 14 miles of Grade 2 land.

- Regeneration: High Speed Two would support regeneration initiatives at Euston, Old Oak Common and in central Birmingham.

5.50 The Government and HS2 Ltd are mindful of their obligations in respect of protected habitats and species at international, national and local levels, and are aware of the general duty to protect biodiversity contained in Section 40 of the Natural Environment and Rural Communities Act 2006. HS2 Ltd will, in conjunction with the relevant statutory agencies, continue to investigate any potential impacts of its recommended route, in order to identify and assess possible ways of mitigating these. This will form part of its ongoing development of the proposed line to prepare for formal public consultation later this year.

5.51 Subject to completion of this work and to the results of consultation, the Government's view is that the wider sustainability impacts of the HS2 Line are broadly acceptable, and that it is a therefore a viable project in sustainability terms.

A Eurostar travelling on High Speed One, alongside sound insulating walls and embankments

High Speed Two – Costs and Value for Money

5.52 High Speed Two's benefits for the economy and society need to be set against its costs in order to assess whether it would offer good value for money.

5.53 HS2 Ltd has estimated the present value cost of High Speed Two as around £25.5 billion at 2009 prices. Because these costs would be incurred in the future, a 'discount rate' of 3.5 per cent for the first 30 years and 3 per cent thereafter has been applied to derive this figure. This is in line with HM Treasury guidance and reflects the fact that benefits and costs today are more highly valued than those in the future.

5.54 This overall figure is derived from a number of elements including infrastructure costs for the design and construction of the High Speed Two line itself, plus the cost of rolling stock and also the longer term costs of the operation, maintenance and renewal of the line. HS2 Ltd's report explains how it has derived its cost estimates in more detail.

5.55 As well as the costs of HS2 Ltd's proposed line, the long term revenues that it would generate, mainly from fares, also need to be considered. These are estimated as totalling around £15 billion over the 60 year appraisal period. Again, this figure is at 2009 prices and discounted according to HM Treasury guidance. It is derived on the basis of the demand forecasts summarised above and an assumption that fares on High Speed Two would be broadly comparable with those charged on the existing conventional network for the same journey.

London to Birmingham

5.56 Taken together, and following further, largely technical, adjustments, HS2 Ltd calculates that these give a net cost to Government over 60 years of £11.9 billion at 2009 prices.

5.57 The estimated value of High Speed Two's benefits is derived from the assessment of the time savings delivered to its passengers (in comparison to the journey times they would have experienced had they made their journeys via existing networks), and improvements in crowding and reliability.

5.58 HS2 Ltd has assessed the potential transport benefits which would accrue from High Speed Two over 60 years as totalling approximately £28.7 billion at 2009 prices.

5.59 Alongside these transport benefits, there would be benefits as a result of overall improvements in safety, air quality and noise due to passengers shifting their journeys from other modes of transport, which HS2 Ltd calculates total less than £0.1 billion. In line with the overall assessment of carbon impacts as broadly neutral, no provision has been made by HS2 Ltd in its value for money assessment for changes in carbon emissions.

5.60 These costs and benefits are summarised in Table 5.1. It shows an overall benefit:cost ratio of around 2.4:1. This is well in excess of the Department for Transport's 2:1 threshold for high value for money.

Table 5.1 Present Value Costs and Benefits of HS2*

	Business	Other
(1) Transport User Benefits	£17.6bn	£11.1bn
(2) Other Benefits (excl. Carbon)	Less than £0.1bn	
(3) Net Transport Benefits (PVB) = (1) + (2)	£28.7bn	
(4) Capital Costs	£17.8bn	
(5) Operating Costs	£7.6bn	
(6) Total Costs = (4) + (5)	£25.5bn	
(7) Revenues	£15bn	
(8) Indirect Taxes	-£1.5bn	
(9) Net Costs to Government (PVC) = (6) − (7) − (8)	£11.9bn	
(10) NATA** Benefit Cost Ratio = (3) ÷ (9)	2.4	

* (PV2009 discount year and prices)
** NATA is the DfTs standard appraisal method which provides estimates of all the impacts of a scheme and expresses most of the main ones in money values to provide a benefit cost ratio (NATA BCR).

5.61 This assessment follows the Department for Transport's standard New Approach to Appraisal (NATA) methodology, and therefore does not include other potential benefits, such as the project's wider economic impacts, as discussed in Chapter Three. If these wider economic impacts are included in the assessment the benefit:cost ratio increases to 2.7:1.

5.62 There would also be additional impacts for which monetisation poses significant challenges, but which still need to be taken into account – in particular the proposed line's effects on landscape, biodiversity and heritage set out above. In addition, noise impacts can only be monetised to a limited extent. From the Government's initial assessment, it does not, however, believe that these would alter its overall conclusion that High Speed Two would offer high value for money.

5.63 The Government has assessed HS2 Ltd's calculation of the costs and benefits of its proposed high speed line, and considers that it is robust and has been carried out fully in accordance with HM Treasury and NATA guidance. It notes both High Speed Two's potential non-monetised impacts on the local environment, and the wider economic benefits that it could deliver. On that basis, it agrees with HS2 Ltd that it is likely that High Speed Two would deliver high value for money, with more than £2 of benefits provided for every £1 spent.

The Government's Assessment

5.64 HS2 Ltd's work has demonstrated that a British high speed line, based on tried and tested technologies, built to European standards and future-proofed to accommodate future growth in demand and technological changes, could be a credible, buildable project. The Government's assessment is that HS2 Ltd's work has shown that its proposed high speed line from London to Birmingham, High Speed Two, would offer high value for money, delivering more than £2 of benefits for every £1 spent.

5.65 In recommending a viable London terminus and route out of the city, it has met one of the most significant challenges that any north-south high speed line faces. By providing substantial capacity increases on a key rail corridor north from the capital, such a line would provide the foundation for a wider network, whilst at the same time enabling services to be run beyond Birmingham from the outset by linking to existing lines.

5.66 The Government's view is that High Speed Two should be planned from the start to form the foundation for a wider core high speed rail network extending to Manchester and Leeds. It has asked HS2 Ltd to undertake similar detailed planning work on the routes from Birmingham to those cities, to be completed in summer 2011, with a view to formal consultation beginning in early 2012.

5.67 The following chapters provide a more detailed explanation of the specific issues considered by HS2 Ltd in their design of their recommended route, the conclusions they reached, and the Government's response in each case, including where it has commissioned further work on particular topics.

6. High Speed Two – The Route

6.1 This chapter describes HS2 Ltd's recommended route for a new high speed line from London to the West Midlands ("High Speed Two"). It sets out the options that HS2 Ltd considered in reaching its recommendations, and the Government's response.

London Terminus

6.2 Building a city centre high speed rail station would be particularly challenging in London: a historic and densely developed metropolis in which existing rail corridors and stations are close to operational capacity and where new development sites are at a premium.

6.3 The size of the extension necessary to accommodate international high speed services at St Pancras – hitherto a much under-utilised station – demonstrates the scale of footprint required for 400 metre long high speed trains. The trains using High Speed Two would be similar in length to those on Eurostar services, and substantially larger than any trains currently operating on the conventional network, in some cases carrying over 1,000 passengers. This would create very significant potential demands on connections to urban transport systems including the Underground.

6.4 HS2 Ltd started with an extensive long-list of 27 sites in London. These included inner and outer London locations, as well as surface and underground options. It also tested two alternatives to a single London terminus: either two smaller independent termini or two configurations of a central London through-station. HS2 Ltd applied an iterative short-listing process, in which locations were assessed against criteria including: overall fit with the remit; operational/engineering feasibility; demand (including passenger access times to various locations in London); cost; and planning and environmental constraints. This produced a short list of a surface station at Euston (with three sub-option configurations) and a cut-and-cover station at Kings Cross Lands.

6.5 Of these, a single-level station at Euston was identified as the most promising option on the grounds of construction and operational impact, sustainability, cost and economic case. Furthermore, the existing Euston Station would need to be redeveloped within the timescale of the High Speed Two project even without a new high speed line, due to growth in passenger demand on the West Coast Main Line.

6.6 HS2 Ltd's recommendation is therefore for a redeveloped Euston Station. This station would comprise 10 high speed platforms and 14 classic platforms and would be able to accommodate the proposed new high speed line's long-term maximum service pattern of 18 trains per hour. All platforms would be just below the track level in the existing station. The station's design would allow for an extension of the concourse above the trains to almost the full length of the trains, and would provide ground level accessibility to the concourse from three sides of the station.

6.7 HS2 Ltd noted the potential increase in Underground crowding that would result from high speed rail passengers using Euston. By 2033 it is expected that some 200,000 passengers will be travelling through Euston on London Underground services during the three-hour morning peak, with West Coast Main Line services into Euston contributing a further 24,000 passengers even without High Speed Two. The case therefore, for an additional Crossrail Interchange to relieve pressure at Euston, whilst enhancing High Speed Two's connectivity, is compelling. Assuming that a Crossrail Interchange station is provided, High Speed Two would add only another 4,000 Underground passengers at Euston, beyond the 24,000 forecast above. In further developing its plans, HS2 Ltd proposes to work with Transport for London and Network Rail on options for managing the interface with London Underground and other local transport at Euston Station.

6.8 There would also be significant redevelopment potential at Euston and in the surrounding area, due to the enlarged station footprint and the subsurface location of the rebuilt platforms and track. HS2 Ltd has noted the significant potential for residential, recreational, retail and commercial development as part of a Euston Station rebuild, akin to the redevelopment now taking place at nearby Kings Cross and St Pancras, together with the opportunity to reconnect communities on either side of the existing station.

6.9 The benefits to local communities of a well-designed and managed redevelopment could be substantial, as described by Sir Terry Farrell later in this chapter. However, the Government also recognises that any development at Euston would have some adverse impact for a number of local residents, particularly while construction is underway. HS2 Ltd's proposed station footprint would require the demolition of a number of buildings, including five blocks of flats currently mainly occupied by Camden Council tenants. It would be a priority to ensure that clear and appropriate proposals were agreed for suitable re-accommodation of people affected in this way, including, if Camden Council so wish, considering rehousing options on-site as part of the redevelopment. HS2 Ltd proposes to work with Camden Council and local residents on a suitable masterplan for the site.

Proposed footprint of expanded Euston Station, to accommodate high speed and conventional trains

High Speed Rail

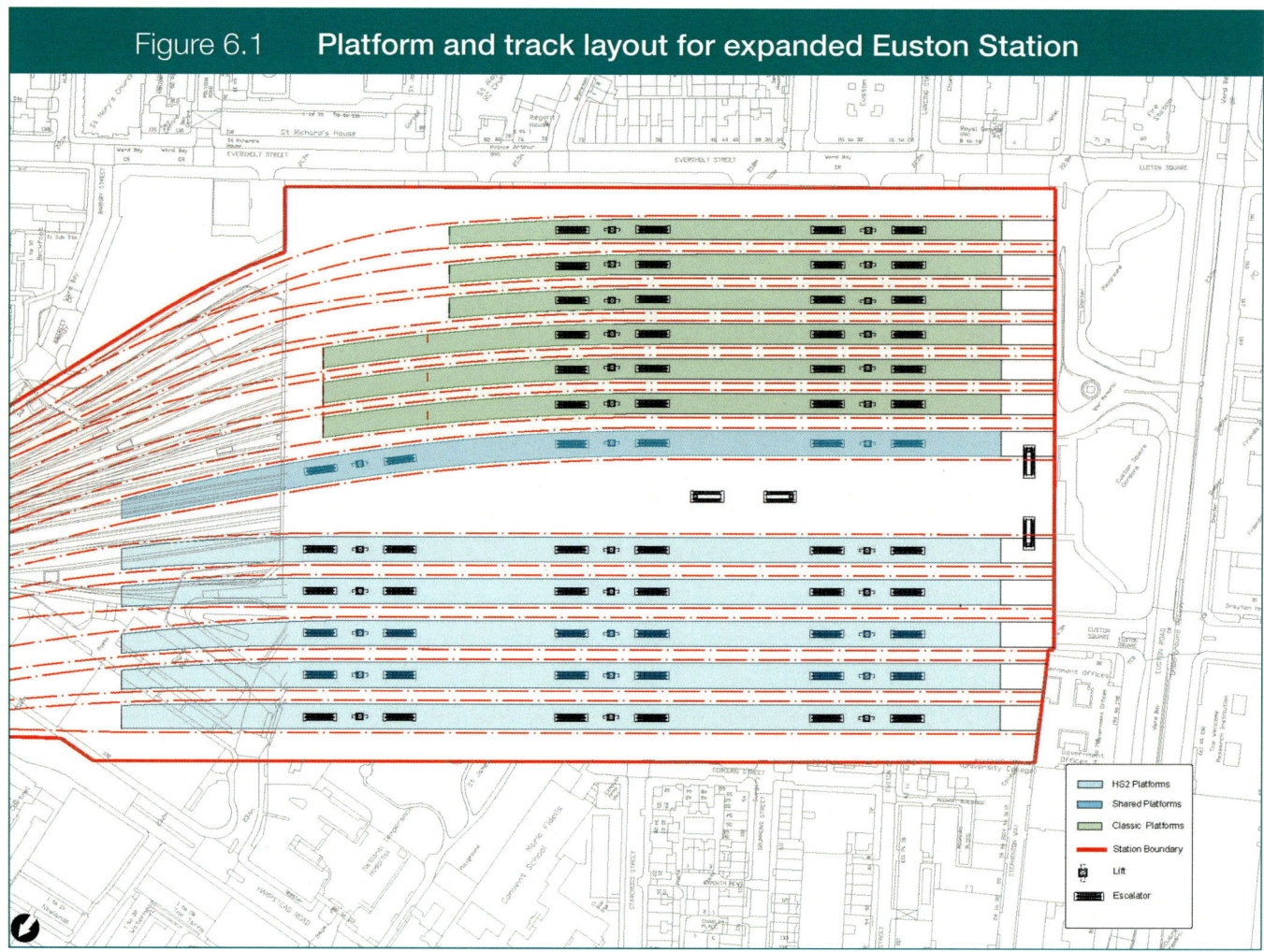

Figure 6.1   Platform and track layout for expanded Euston Station

6.10   The Government would expect that the funding package for any redevelopment would include appropriate contributions from those organisations benefiting from it.

6.11   Redevelopment of Euston Station would also directly affect rail passengers both as a result of the physical construction work and through any disruption to existing train services. Initial work by HS2 Ltd has identified various ways in which such disruption could be substantially mitigated, and it does not anticipate the need for any extended closures or for the construction of a temporary station – as was required at St Pancras. Identifying optimum construction phasing would form part of the future detailed design work, involving HS2 Ltd, Network Rail and Transport for London, and can be expected to take several years.

6.12   Subject to the considerations set out above, and to public consultation, the Government agrees with HS2 Ltd's recommendation that a London terminus for the new high speed rail line should be provided by redeveloping Euston Station.

Crossrail Interchange

6.13 A central London terminus for High Speed Two is essential. However, in addition to the capacity considerations described above, Euston is also limited in its connectivity. It has direct connections only to the Northern and Victoria Underground lines, and relatively poor connectivity for those making east-west journeys.

6.14 Valuable connectivity – as well as capacity – benefits would flow from a High Speed Two interchange with the new east-west Crossrail line, which will run from west of Paddington through to the West End, the City of London, Canary Wharf and into Essex, and will include a link to Heathrow.

6.15 A Crossrail Interchange station would (according to HS2 Ltd's modelling) benefit about a third of all High Speed Two passengers, who would use the Crossrail Interchange in preference to Euston, relieving pressure on the Victoria and Northern lines. This interchange could also provide additional links to services on the Great Western Main Line and Heathrow Express connections to Heathrow Airport.

6.16 Having considered several potential sites, HS2 Ltd has recommended a Crossrail Interchange station on railway land a short distance west of Paddington at Old Oak Common in West London. This would enable the station to be developed on a site currently used for depots and sidings, substantially limiting its potential impacts on the local environment and communities. The site is also in an area of London identified as a priority for regeneration, to which the development of a new interchange station could make a major contribution.

6.17 From a construction perspective, HS2 Ltd advise that Old Oak Common is the only site in West London suitable for launching the tunnel boring machines needed to create the tunnels needed for High Speed Two to reach Euston. This substantially reduces the additional cost of providing an interchange station on the site, as some of the major excavations will be needed whether a station is built or not.

6.18 An interchange station at Old Oak Common would provide good connections for passengers between High Speed Two, Crossrail, the Great Western Main Line and the Heathrow Express. It would have the potential to be served by up to 24 Crossrail services per hour giving passengers a fast, high frequency, high capacity service to key business destinations in the West End, the City and Docklands.

Sir Terry Farrell: Opportunities for cities and place-making

As an architect and town planner, I believe in the potential of stations to transform cities.

Across the globe in countries such as Japan, Korea, and China – and in most European countries – there is a strong commitment to high speed rail and expansion of high speed networks. I have been involved in designing and building some of the world's largest railway stations and transport interchange buildings. As an architect and town planner my own particular focus has been on cities and place-making rather than on route planning and train technology *per se*. To me, the potential of stations to transform cities is critically important.

High speed rail stations are so much more than points of arrival and departure. They create whole new districts – places defined by their connectedness to other city centres and to airports, ports and metropolitan transport infrastructure. They become accumulators and attractors for all movement systems including underground rail, buses, taxis, pedestrians and cyclists.

They also attract people and new investment. In the projects that I have been involved in, high speed rail stations attract new businesses, office development, hotels and conference centres. They become desirable new residential districts, and they present civic opportunities for new public squares, cultural activity and recreation. Stations have become pre-eminent in their role as place-makers.

This is all a far cry from the origins of rail in the nineteenth century, where it was initially associated with goods transportation. Early stations sat within an environment of coal yards, gas works, factories, breweries, warehouses and industrial canal basins. In the UK many of our primary rail stations were built in the industrial era, so in most major cities stations were built on the periphery in areas of low value, set apart from the vibrancy of city life.

But 21st century train travel is essentially people-based, and the best systems combine the inherent civility of train travel with the standards of efficiency, modernity and cleanliness to be found in high quality air travel. The critical advantage is that these can be integrated within the heart of our city centres rather than banished to places where noise and pollution impacts are less important.

Properly designed, stations become magnificent expressions of civic endeavour. The best have concourses that are grand halls with thriving restaurants, meeting places and other amenities. It is said that within the new St Pancras station 40% of the people there at any given time are there for reasons other than travel.

In Hong Kong our Kowloon Station development has attracted high value development more than twice the size of Canary Wharf. The focus of this new place is a grand station square set within Kowloon on what was the less favoured side of Victoria Harbour. The station complex – which includes a high speed rail link to Guangzhou – has generated city-wide change and will in time become one of the largest land transportation hubs in the Far East. It will have Asia's largest cultural district and some of its finest buildings (including some of its tallest and most valuable).

Our Beijing South Station was deliberately planned from the outset as a whole new centre within the capital city, with a new metro serving a new mixed use commercial district. The centre of this new district is the station itself with a vast hall twice the size of that at Grand Central Station in New York. The extent to which high quality stations embody civic pride and city-making is reflected in the fact that Beijing South Station won a recent public poll as the city's favourite building amongst a list that included the 'Bird's Nest' Olympic Arena and the National Opera House. It gained 3,500,000 votes.

Of course, some of the circumstances are different in Britain, but the principles still apply. The UK's new high speed rail stations would transform all their destinations. We can already see how the emerging new city at Stratford in East London – the base of the 2012 London Olympics – and the new international station at St Pancras have revolutionised different parts of London. This effect would be repeated all over the UK wherever high speed rail arrives and departs. The greatest value of high speed rail could be its effect on cities and towns and their economies.

In London, the new terminus at Euston Station could become one of the greatest stations in the world. The proposals include not only new platforms but also a remodelled and expanded tube station and dedicated bus and taxi interchanges providing direct and seamless access to the station concourse.

It would be much more than one new station. A new dedicated pedestrian link could connect Euston Station to St Pancras and Kings Cross to become Europe's 'super rail hub'. It is estimated that together these stations will carry more than 250 million passengers per annum in the long run. By comparison, London's three main airports carry less than half of this number today.

With the regeneration at Kings Cross, station development at Euston would create potential for development at least equal in scale to Canary Wharf.

It would become the most vibrant and cosmopolitan new district in London as well as its most connected, forming as it does part of the Marylebone – Euston Road corridor which extends west to Paddington Station, with its national and international connections including the Heathrow Express.

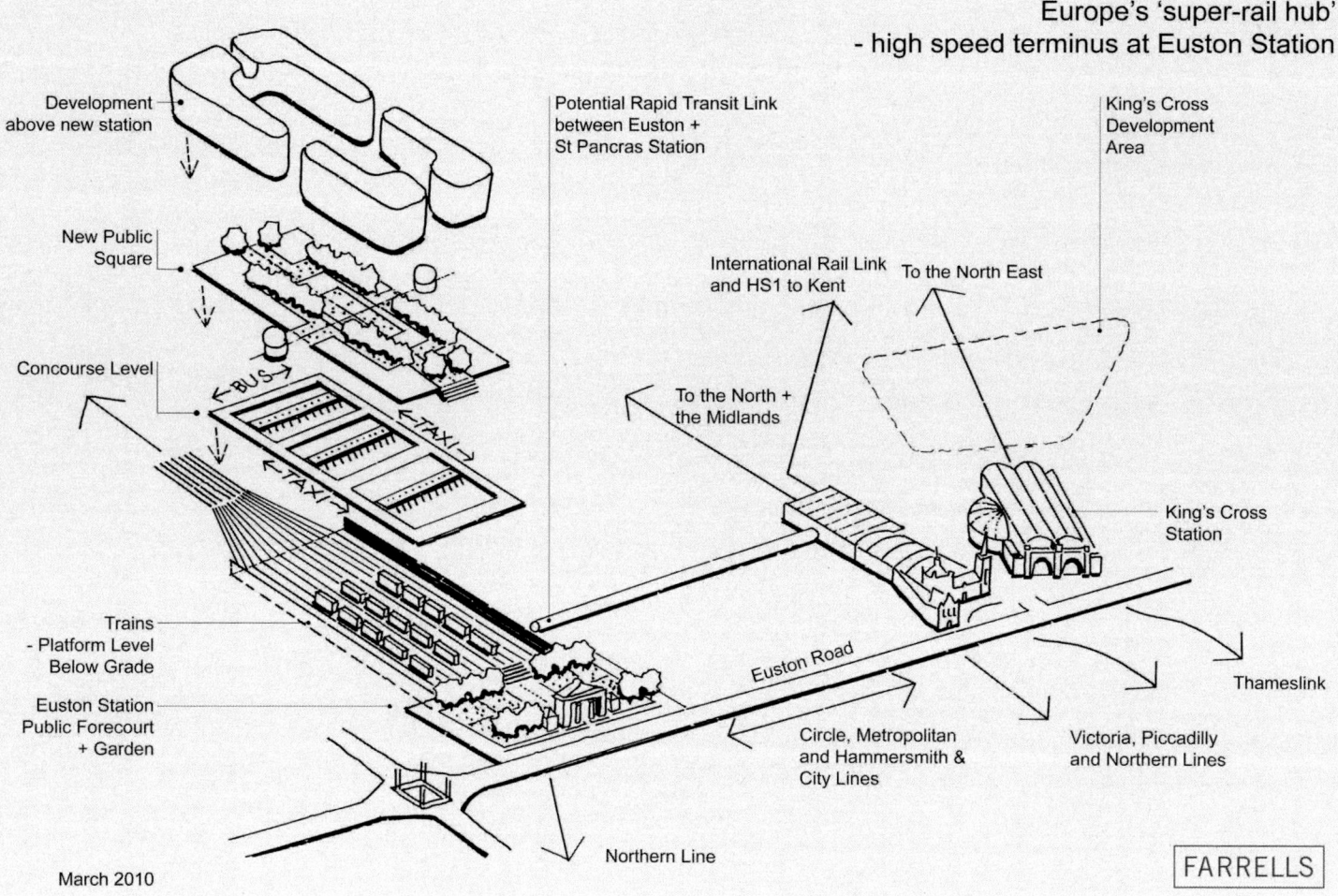

Since the new platforms would be almost two stories below ground level, the new Euston would allow the introduction of new streets and public squares which improve east-west connections, notoriously difficult at present given the current station design. It would allow much better resolution of the interchange between rail, bus and taxi, and on Euston Road there is an opportunity to create a London square fit for the 21st century. I support the return of a reconstructed Euston Arch at the station's front door.

In Birmingham the new high speed station would be similarly revolutionary in its impact. The new hub would improve interchange between the three stations (including Birmingham New Street and Moor Street stations).

It would improve the setting of the new award winning shopping centre at the Bullring, and improve connectivity to the city's central area via New Street to Victoria and Chamberlain Squares, the city's civic heart. Rail could reinforce Birmingham's commitment to an improved pedestrian experience in the city centre, a far cry from the city's vision of itself as the motor car city of the 1960s and 1970s.

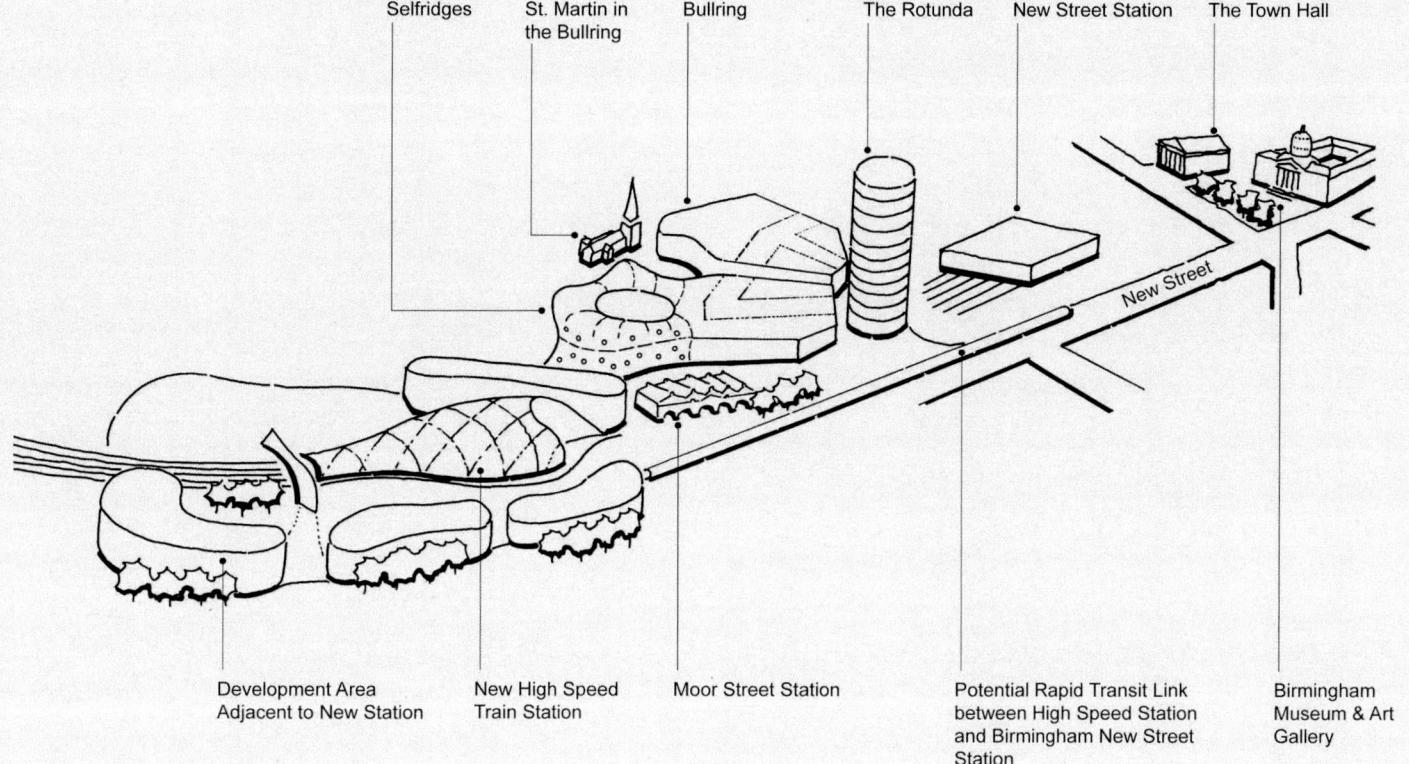

Birmingham City Centre High Speed Station

Labels: Selfridges; St. Martin in the Bullring; Bullring; The Rotunda; New Street Station; The Town Hall; Development Area Adjacent to New Station; New High Speed Train Station; Moor Street Station; Potential Rapid Transit Link between High Speed Station and Birmingham New Street Station; Birmingham Museum & Art Gallery

March 2010

FARRELLS

The new rail hub would also form the centrepiece of a major regeneration and development area in East Birmingham. This would be around 45 minutes from London's West End, making East Birmingham more accessible to central London than some of the London Boroughs on the metropolitan periphery. This accessibility would undoubtedly help to attract new investment to the city and the Midlands generally.

Both London and Birmingham would also have much improved connections to airport interchanges by means of stations at Birmingham International (also improving access to the National Exhibition Centre) and a Crossrail Interchange station in West London (which would also connect to the existing national rail network and Heathrow Express, acting as a catalyst for regeneration and development in this relatively underperforming part of West London).

High speed rail represents a great opportunity to re-think cities and place-making. New high speed stations are potentially the most exciting opportunities for our cities at this time.

Sir Terry Farrell CBE

High Speed Rail

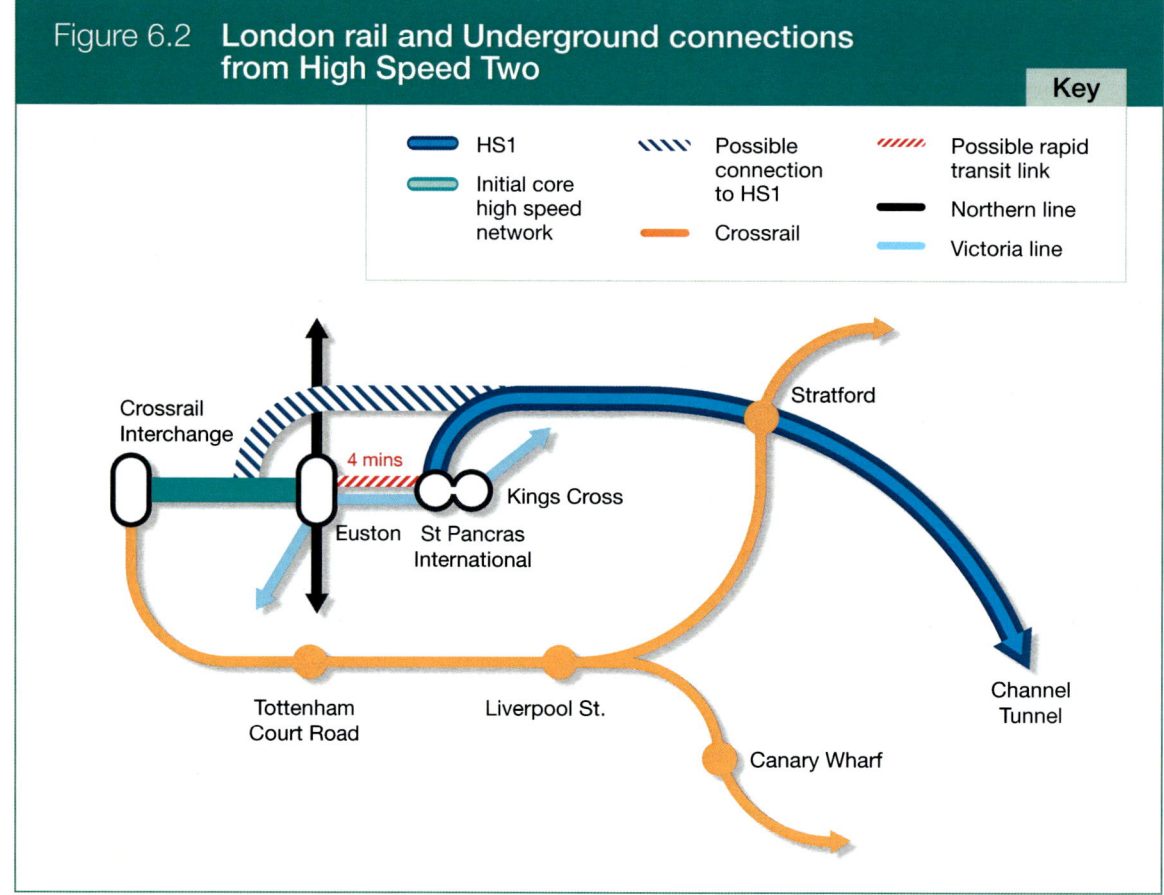

Figure 6.2 London rail and Underground connections from High Speed Two

6.19 Connections between High Speed Two and other lines at the Crossrail Interchange would be fast and convenient. In contrast to Euston, where access to the Underground is some distance from the main line platforms, HS2 Ltd's proposed design locates the Crossrail, Heathrow Express and Great Western Main Line platforms very close to those serving High Speed Two.

6.20 Through the connection with services on the Great Western Main Line, HS2 Ltd's proposal would provide opportunities for passengers from West London and the Thames Valley to reach the Midlands and the North on High Speed Two without having to travel via Central London and Euston. For other Great Western Main Line passengers, this interchange station may provide a quicker and easier link to Crossrail than changing trains at Paddington. This could help to reduce the number of passengers interchanging between high and low level platforms at Paddington.

6.21 The Crossrail Interchange station would also facilitate fast and convenient connections to High Speed Two and Crossrail for Great Western travellers from Bristol, the South West and South Wales. It would also provide a connection to direct Heathrow Express services to and from Terminals 1, 2, 3 and 5 at Heathrow Airport. This would enable Heathrow to be served economically and efficiently using existing infrastructure, alongside any potential future extension of the high speed rail network to include an at-airport station at Heathrow.

High Speed Two – The Route

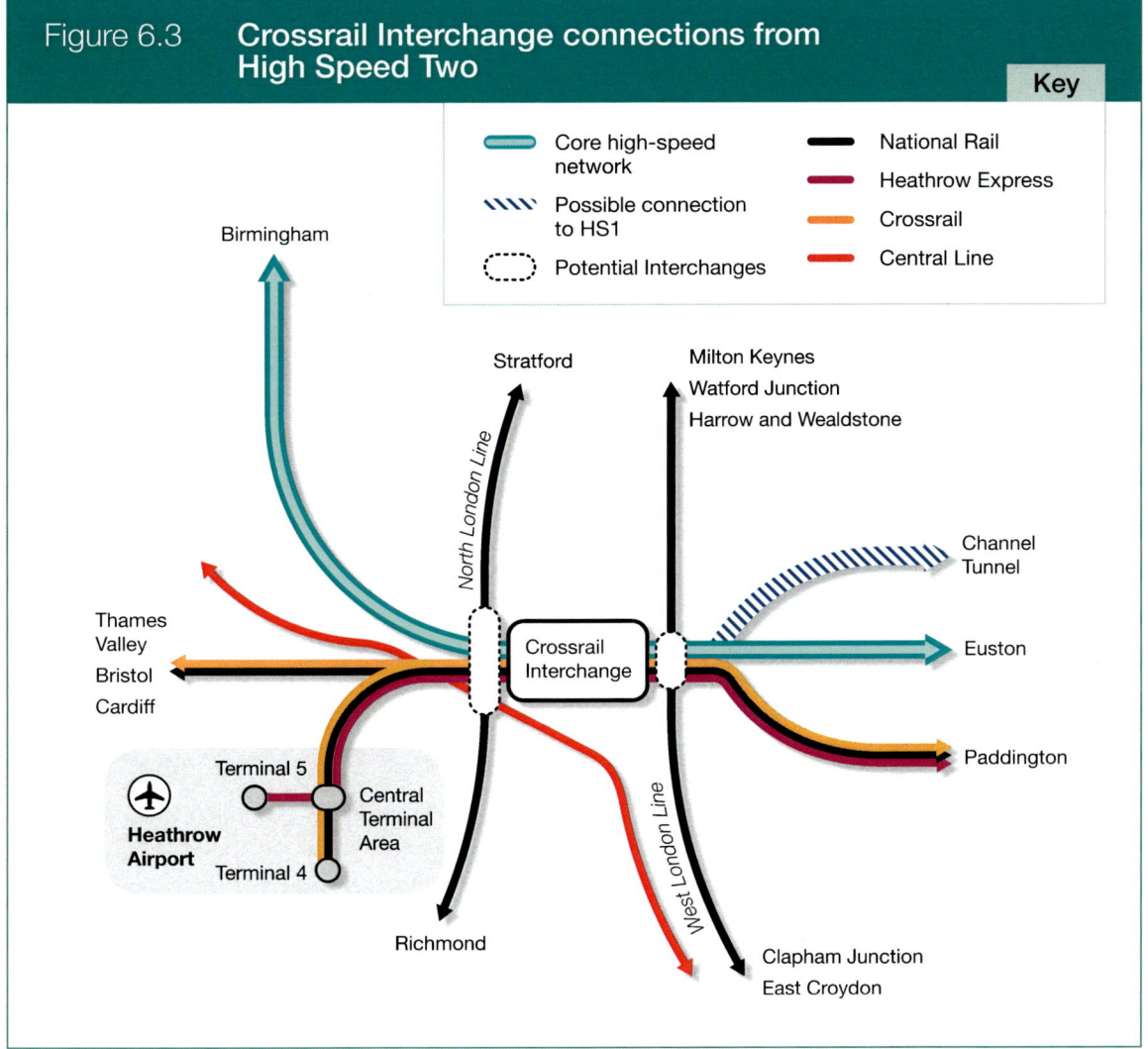

Figure 6.3 Crossrail Interchange connections from High Speed Two

6.22 BAA is currently promoting the Heathrow Airtrack project to provide new rail links to Heathrow Airport from Surrey, Berkshire and South West London. As part of this proposal, alternate Heathrow Express services would run beyond Heathrow Terminal 5 to Staines where connections would be made with the South West suburban rail network. If approved and implemented, these services would further widen the catchment area of the Crossrail Interchange station and avoid the need for passengers to travel via Central London.

6.23 As well as significantly reducing pressure at Euston, HS2 Ltd's analysis suggests that the high levels of accessibility offered by a Crossrail Interchange station at Old Oak Common would attract up to seven per cent more passengers to use High Speed Two services than if no comparable interchange was provided, and would deliver net benefits of some £2 billion.

6.24 The Crossrail Interchange station proposal also has further long term potential to provide connections with other rail routes passing close to the site. It could enable passenger access from wide areas of London by means of London Overground services. Although somewhat further from

107

the proposed Crossrail Interchange site, the Central and Bakerloo lines also pass through the area and may have the potential to be linked in to a wider redevelopment project.

6.25 The Government believes that the proposed Crossrail Interchange station could act as a catalyst to transform the current brownfield area and surrounding neighbourhoods and could provide major employment and housing opportunities. As the site is already largely used for railway purposes, any adverse environmental impacts resulting from the development would be limited.

6.26 HS2 Ltd notes that serving a Crossrail Interchange station would lengthen journey times for through passengers both on High Speed Two and Great Western Main Line services. However, as the site of the proposed Crossrail Interchange is close to Central London in an area where both High Speed Two and Great Western line speeds are relatively low, the additional journey time resulting from calling at the station would be fairly small – around four minutes for through passengers on High Speed Two. As noted above, HS2 Ltd's assessment shows that the overall benefits to passengers as a result of the proposed interchange far outweigh these longer journey times to the extent that net benefits of some £2 billion are generated.

6.27 The Government accepts HS2 Ltd's recommendations in respect of a Crossrail Interchange station, because of its key role in integrating High Speed Two with London's transport networks, enhancing connectivity, facilitating passengers' end-to-end journeys and helping to relieve crowding on London Underground services at Euston. The Government expects that the existing Crossrail scheme will continue to be delivered as defined and will open from 2017. Over the coming months, HS2 Ltd will undertake further detailed work, in collaboration with Crossrail and its sponsors – the Department for Transport and Transport for London – as well as with Hammersmith and Fulham Council to develop more detailed plans for a Crossrail Interchange station, which will form part of the formal public consultation on the route.

6.28 Subject to that consultation, further work will be required by HS2 Ltd in conjunction with Transport for London, the relevant London Boroughs, Network Rail and other stakeholders to develop an overall plan for the Old Oak Common area which will maximise the benefits for passengers and take full advantage of the wider development potential of the site and surrounding areas. The Government expects that the funding package for the Crossrail Interchange would include equitable contributions from those who would benefit from this redevelopment.

The Route from Central London to the West Midlands

6.29 The challenge in finding a route out of London is the obvious one of threading a high speed line through a dense urban landscape. As set out in the box below, balancing the significant costs and impacts of tunnelling with the noise and other impacts on communities from a surface route is a difficult judgement. This has been a major concern for HS2 Ltd in its recommendations on the options for the route to Birmingham.

> Tunnelling involves significantly higher and more uncertain costs than a surface alignment, and is not without environmental impact: in terms of higher 'embedded' carbon in construction; the need to dispose of a substantial volume of excavated material; the need for surface works for ventilation purposes; and the (relatively small) risk of surface properties being affected by subsidence during construction and by ground-borne noise and vibration afterwards. Nor are long tunnelled sections desirable from an operational perspective. On the other hand, a surface route can have visual and noise impacts, may require compulsory purchases and demolitions of property, and may cause severance if it creates a new transport corridor.

6.30 HS2 Ltd has taken into account the need for effective integration between High Speed Two and existing urban, national and international networks, through direct connections with key London transport networks, including Crossrail and the Heathrow Express. For these reasons, HS2 Ltd has focused on routes leading out of London to the north west and west. In considering the options presented by HS2 Ltd, the Government has also borne in mind their potential to allow a direct connection to an at-airport station at Heathrow in future.

6.31 HS2 Ltd's preferred route from Euston is a tunnelled section running from just north of the terminus to Old Oak Common, which is proposed as the site for the Crossrail Interchange station. After departing the Crossrail Interchange station, HS2 Ltd's recommended route would leave London via the Ruislip area, making use of an existing rail corridor.

6.32 Having left London, the most direct route to Birmingham would pass through the Chiltern Hills. The challenge for HS2 Ltd, therefore, has been to design options for this section of the route as sensitively as possible and, in particular, to minimise any potential impacts on the Chilterns Area of Outstanding Natural Beauty (AONB).

6.33 As part of its route evaluation process, HS2 Ltd considered two routes that largely avoided the Chilterns AONB. These options, which sought to follow the routes of the M1 and Midland Main Line, were discounted after analysis by HS2 Ltd. Their alignments would be less direct, resulting in longer journey times; and they would involve the need for significantly more demolition than other routes, including of residential properties, unless substantial and expensive tunnelling was undertaken to reduce the impacts on major towns such as Luton and Dunstable. The Government also notes that their routes through Hertfordshire and Luton would be much too far to the east for a link to an at-airport station at Heathrow to be remotely feasible.

> Following close to existing motorway alignments could provide an opportunity to reduce some of the potential impacts of a new high speed rail line. However, because high speed rail requires shallower curves than either conventional rail or motorways, it would not be possible for a new line to follow many existing routes without requiring either frequent speed restrictions which would undermine the core benefit of high speed rail or, alternatively, blighting significant 'islands' of countryside by isolating them between the curves of the road alignment and the necessarily straighter railway. This would be true of both the M1 and M40.

6.34 HS2 Ltd therefore concluded that any viable line of route between London and Birmingham would, subject to management of its local and environmental impacts, necessarily traverse some part of the Chilterns. From the six main corridors through the Chilterns, HS2 Ltd short-listed three potential routes:

- A route leaving London via the existing Chiltern Line corridor to Ruislip, and then using a combination of tunnelling and the existing A413 corridor to reduce impacts on the Chiltern AONB (HS2 Ltd's 'Route 3');

- A route following the same corridor to Ruislip, but then passing in tunnel beneath Gerrards Cross before crossing the Chiltern AONB through a combination of tunnelling and surface routes including a 720 metre viaduct across the Hughenden Valley (HS2 Ltd's 'Route 2.5');

- A route leaving London via a 28-kilometre tunnel towards Kings Langley, before passing through the Chilterns AONB and close to the town of Berkhamsted (HS2 Ltd's 'Route 4').

6.35 HS2 Ltd assessed the operational and environmental effects of these three options. This led it to recommend following the A413 transport corridor (Route 3). This route is shorter and would provide a faster journey time than either of the others. It also offers, overall, a number of sustainability and environmental advantages over the other options. Furthermore, its estimated cost of £3.7 billion (without provision for risk) is significantly lower than the alternatives (HS2 Ltd estimate the costs of Route 2.5 at £4.3 billion and of Route 4 at £5.1 billion without risk).

6.36 The Government agrees with HS2 Ltd that the route via Kings Langley is inferior, due to its slower journey times and the considerably higher costs entailed in constructing a route entirely in tunnel out of London to the M25. The total length of tunnel from Euston to Kings Langley would be around 22 miles – over two thirds the length of the Channel Tunnel. By leaving London to the north west, it would also effectively preclude the future provision of a link to an at-airport station at Heathrow.

6.37 The Government has carefully evaluated the choice between the A413 and Hughenden Valley routes, and considers that, as well as its cost and journey time advantages, the A413 route's local and environmental impacts are on balance lower than those of the Hughenden Valley route. The A413 route has lower impacts in respect of its potential for isolation of existing settlements and ground-borne noise. Its environmental impacts are reduced by following existing transport corridors, including the busy A413 itself, for well over half the distance travelled at surface level through the AONB; and by reducing visual intrusion through the use of cuttings and screening with vegetation and embankments.

6.38 In contrast, although the Hughenden Valley route's surface sections through the Chilterns AONB are shorter than those of the A413 route, they would have other potentially significant impacts, including on townscape and landscape setting, as there is no major existing transport corridor that this route can follow to reduce its negative impacts. A major viaduct would be required to cross the Hughenden Valley itself, with significant visual, townscape and environmental implications for the surrounding area. Other impacts associated with the proposed tunnels on this route include greater energy expenditure, larger quantities of spoil, and greater potential vibration impacts, and it would also require more land take and more potential demolitions than the A413 route.

6.39 North of the Chilterns, the A413 route would pass Aylesbury before following the largely preserved track-bed of the former Great Central Railway until Brackley. Other than a short length of line running close to the edge of Aylesbury, for which the Government has asked HS2 Ltd to assess options to mitigate the noise impacts, this section of the A413 route presents few significant impacts on communities or key environmental features. Conversely, the alignment of the Hughenden Valley route prior to Brackley would follow close to the current Chiltern Line for some of its length but would also have sections passing through open countryside without following any existing transport corridor.

6.40 Both the A413 route and the Hughenden Valley route follow the same alignment after Brackley. This runs through open countryside into Warwickshire using cuttings and embankments, due to the area's rolling topography, and passes under the SSSI at Long Itchington Wood in a 1400 metre tunnel. It also runs between the registered Stoneleigh Abbey Park and Garden and the neighbouring National Agricultural Centre. Given its potential impacts on these sites the Government has asked HS2 Ltd to carry out further work to identify the optimum alignment at Stoneleigh.

6.41 Taking account of all these considerations, the Government's assessment is that the route following the A413 corridor would be superior in terms of strategic fit, cost, journey time benefits and overall sustainability impacts, considering the potential for further mitigation. For these reasons, the Government agrees, subject to public consultation and further work on options for mitigating its impacts, with HS2 Ltd's recommendation that the A413 route is the best option, judged against the full range of its objectives.

6.42 The Government is, however, mindful of the need to explore all options for reducing the impacts on the local environment and communities. The initial findings of HS2 Ltd's additional work on route alignments at Aylesbury and Stoneleigh has suggested that its impacts at these places could be reduced.

High Speed Rail

The Government has therefore asked HS2 Ltd to carry out detailed work on these issues and on measures elsewhere to further mitigate noise and other environmental impacts, as the basis for public consultation on this route in the autumn.

Serving Birmingham City Centre

6.43 As with the London terminus, HS2 Ltd evaluated and sifted a range of options in identifying its recommendation for a central Birmingham station and the route through the city to reach it. These included using a new through-station allowing the line from London to run directly through the city centre, as well as a number of options for a station connected to the main high speed line via a short spur, one of which was a redesigned station at Birmingham New Street.

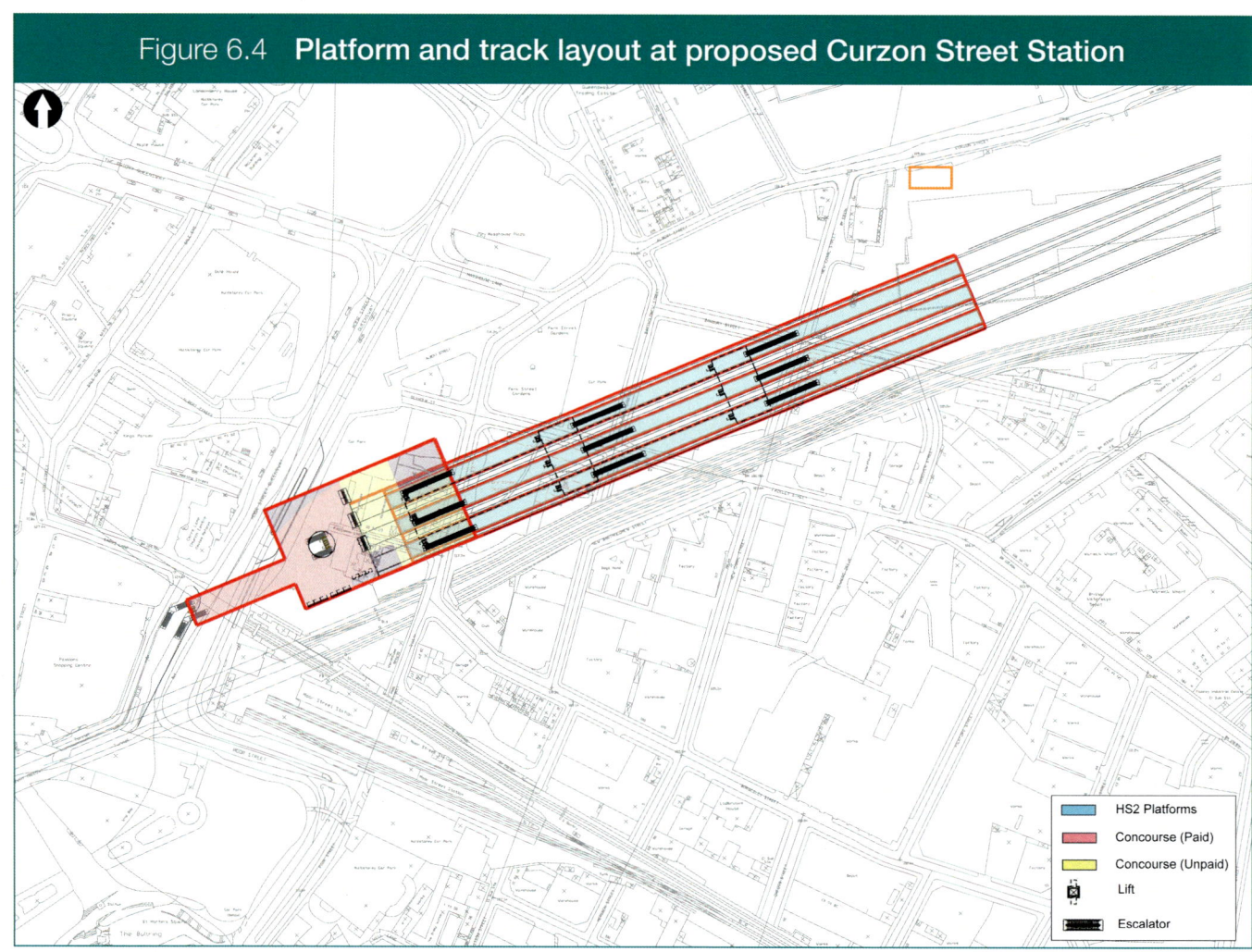

Figure 6.4 **Platform and track layout at proposed Curzon Street Station**

High Speed Two – The Route

6.44 Whilst in principle the option of the high speed line running from London directly through Birmingham city centre appears attractive, none of the options for a through-station was assessed by HS2 Ltd to be workable in practice. Any new through-station would have to be built below surface level, as no appropriate surface site could be identified. This would entail prohibitive costs, relative to other options, and unacceptable townscape and land take impacts.

6.45 There is also little scope for redesigning Birmingham New Street to accommodate high speed services. The station is already operating at close to capacity and is closely bounded by tunnels and city infrastructure, making expansion exceptionally difficult and expensive, and impossible without having to relocate a large number of the existing services to a new station built elsewhere.

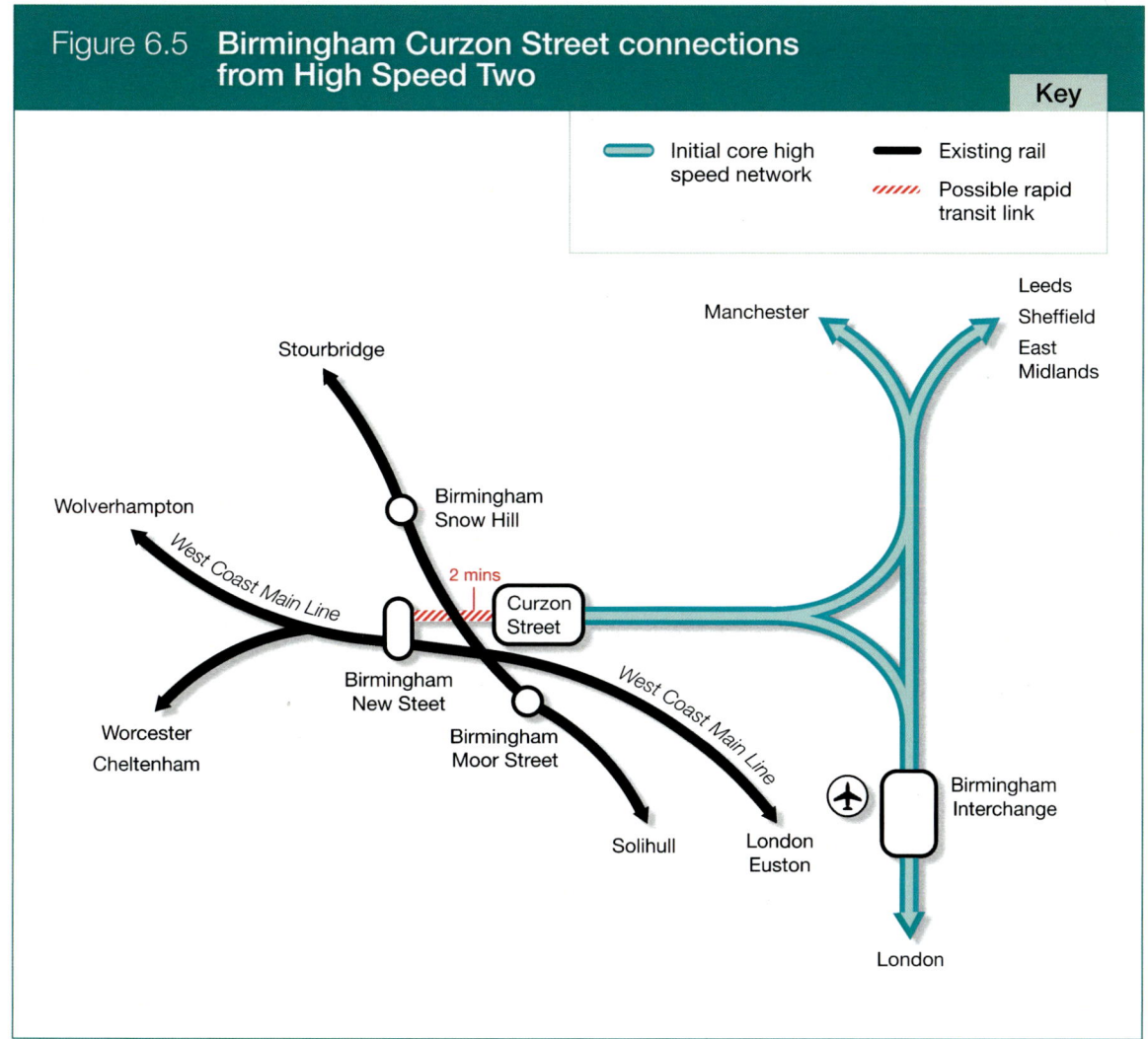

Figure 6.5 Birmingham Curzon Street connections from High Speed Two

6.46 Of the remaining options for a station on a spur line, the two most promising options identified were both for a new station immediately to the east of the city centre and close to Birmingham New Street: either at Curzon/Fazeley Street just to the north of the existing West Coast Main Line, or at Warwick Wharf to the south.

Footprint of proposed Birmingham Curzon Street Station

6.47 The costs of the Curzon/Fazeley Street station would be lower than those of a station at Warwick Wharf, and it would offer marginally quicker journey times. Also, the site on which it would be constructed is mostly vacant and is part of the Eastside area currently identified for redevelopment by Birmingham City Council. Although current plans would need to be revised, a new station at Curzon/Fazeley Street could make a significant contribution to the overall regeneration of the area.

6.48 In contrast, the Warwick Wharf site would be directly within the Warwick Bar Conservation Area, and would substantially affect the street pattern and built character of both that area and the neighbouring Digbeth/Deritend Conservation Area. It would directly impact a number of historic industrial buildings and local landmarks, and affect the setting of several nationally listed buildings.

6.49 For these reasons, the Government agrees, subject to public consultation, with HS2 Ltd's recommendation that the Birmingham terminus should be situated at a new station in the Eastside regeneration area at Curzon/Fazeley Street.

6.50 The Government believes that the station could be constructed as a landmark gateway to Birmingham, with wider redevelopment of the vicinity taking place in parallel, creating exciting new opportunities for the local area, the city and the region more widely. It could incorporate the Grade I listed former station building at Curzon Street, a former Birmingham railway terminus, which is currently unoccupied. It is close to the city centre's shops and other amenities, and has potential for easy and direct access to Birmingham New Street and Moor Street stations, which are currently around a five-minute walk away.

6.51 The Government will start work with Birmingham City Council and other local partners over the coming months to consider how they might take forward this vision, including identifying a package of third party contributions to its costs in line with the benefits that the scheme, if adopted, would generate.

6.52 The location of the Birmingham terminus would also have implications for the route taken by any high speed line through Birmingham and into the city centre. A key advantage of both the Warwick Wharf and Curzon/Fazeley Street sites is that they would enable the high speed line to follow HS2 Ltd's recommended route option running directly east-west from a junction with the main high speed line in the Water Orton area. This option was considered to have lower environmental and social impacts than the alternative route following the West Coast Main Line corridor into the city, as well as ultimately offering faster journey times to locations north of Birmingham.

6.53 HS2 Ltd also recommended that the main high speed line should continue north from Water Orton through the West Midlands to join the West Coast Main Line close to Lichfield, allowing services to continue at conventional speeds to destinations including Manchester, Liverpool and Glasgow.

High Speed Rail

6.54 The Government agrees, subject to public consultation, with HS2 Ltd's recommendations regarding the route into Birmingham and the provision of a link to the West Coast Main Line near Lichfield.

Birmingham Curzon Street Station 1839

The Grade I listed frontage of Birmingham's former Curzon Street terminus was built in 1837 and was intended as a counterpart to the Euston Arch, marking the northern and southern ends respectively of the London and Birmingham Railway. This area of Birmingham included not only the Curzon Street station, but also the Birmingham termini for the Grand Junction Railway from Liverpool and Manchester and the Birmingham and Derby Junction Railway. In 1854, the new through station at New Street was opened, and the Curzon Street station was relegated to handling goods traffic. HS2 Ltd's recommended station option for Birmingham city centre offers an exceptional opportunity to restore this iconic structure to railway use.

Intermediate Stations

6.55 As well as identifying options for city centre stations in London and Birmingham and for an interchange with Crossrail in West London, HS2 Ltd was asked to consider the case for providing an intermediate station between London and the West Midlands – for instance, to provide access to high speed rail services for major towns such as Milton Keynes or Oxford.

6.56 HS2 Ltd examined the potential benefits and disbenefits of such a station and considered a number of options for its location in the light of potential demand. It concluded that an intermediate station between London and the West Midlands would be detrimental to the overall business case.

6.57 The main disbenefits, besides the cost of construction, are the journey time penalties to through passengers and the loss of capacity on the overall high speed network. These arise both through the need to run trains part way with empty seats reserved for passengers joining mid-route, and through the train paths that are foregone as a result of stopping trains on a section of the line that would otherwise be operating at the highest speed. On the latter issue, HS2 Ltd concluded that even with carefully designed junctions and separate approach tracks to and from the intermediate station, the loss of line capacity would still be considerable.

6.58 Furthermore, many of the towns which might benefit from such an intermediate station will already see improvements to existing services on the conventional network over the coming years, such as the benefits for Oxford commuters from investment in the Great Western and Chiltern lines. If High Speed Two was constructed as recommended by HS2 Ltd, many of them, including Milton Keynes, would be likely to benefit from the use of capacity released on the West Coast Main Line as a consequence.

6.59 For these reasons, the Government agrees with HS2 Ltd's recommendation that no intermediate station between London and the West Midlands should be included in the further development of options for the High Speed Two line.

Birmingham Interchange

6.60 HS2 Ltd's analysis indicates that the case for an interchange station in the West Midlands, close to Birmingham Airport, is far more promising. As well as providing enhanced access to the airport for high speed rail passengers, HS2 Ltd's preferred option for such a station would be located close to the M42 and M6 motorways, the existing Birmingham International station and the National Exhibition Centre, improving connectivity for a wide range of travellers to and from the West Midlands.

6.61 HS2 Ltd's modelling indicates that around half of the passengers travelling to and from the West Midlands on High Speed Two would use this station, and that one in six of those would not otherwise have travelled by high speed rail.

6.62 In contrast to an intermediate station between London and the West Midlands, the disbenefits of HS2 Ltd's proposed interchange for other passengers are comparatively modest. This is because the proposed location of such a station close to Birmingham means that there would be relatively little capacity lost as a result of seats occupied by interchange passengers. Trains would also already be slowing to approach Birmingham, reducing the journey time penalties. If any service pattern chosen was to include services that did not stop at the interchange, HS2 Ltd's feasibility work suggests that it would be possible to design the track and junction layout so that they would not be subject to any longer journey times.

High Speed Rail

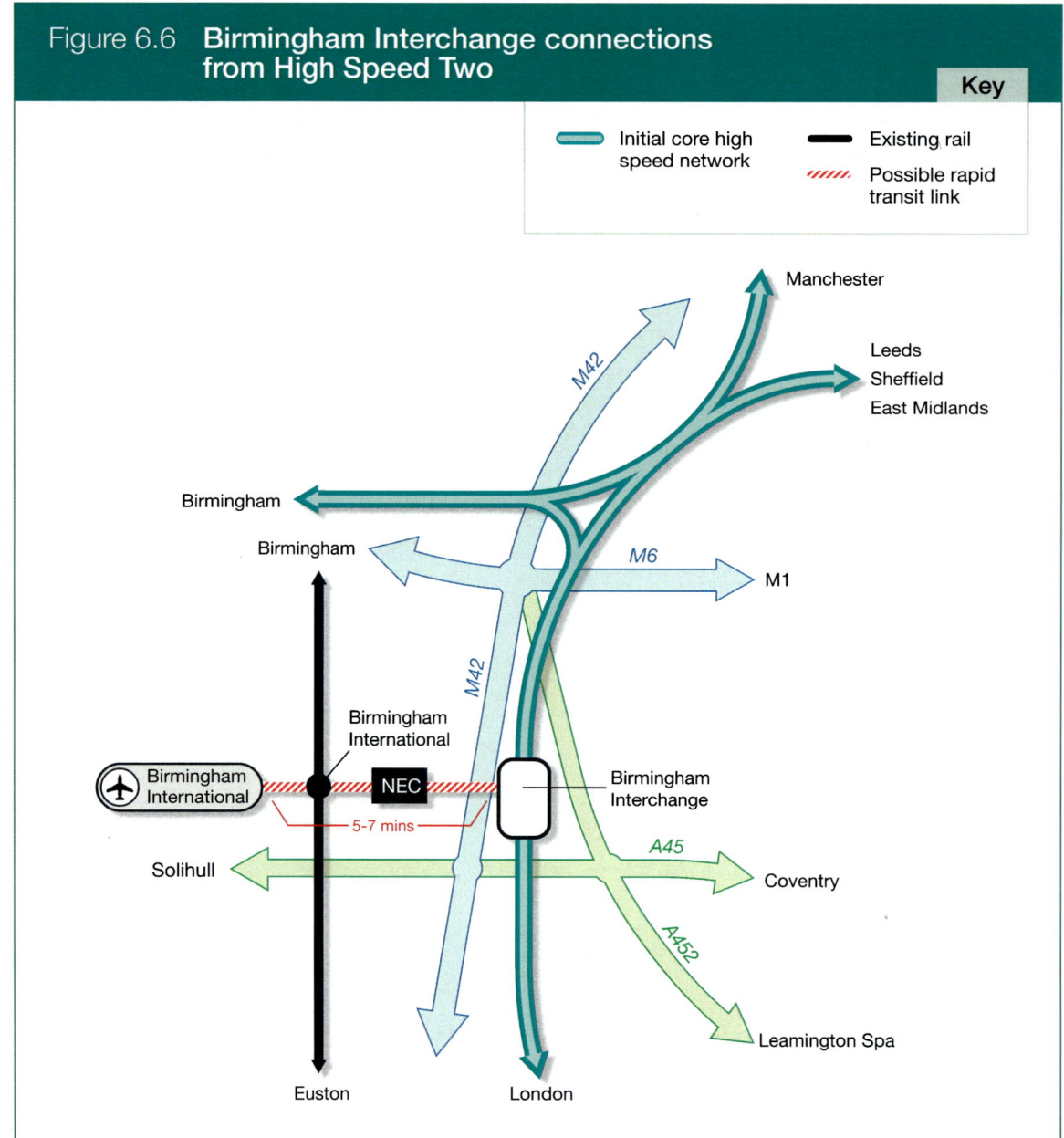

Figure 6.6 Birmingham Interchange connections from High Speed Two

6.63 Although the proposed station would be located within the existing greenbelt, its site also forms part of one of the Major Urban Areas identified in the West Midlands Regional Spatial Strategy, and is bordered on all sides by motorways and airport infrastructure, as well as having previously been proposed as a location for a national football stadium.

6.64 The Government recognises the substantial benefits that an interchange station in the West Midlands could generate, particularly in enhancing connectivity with existing local, national and international transport networks and attracting additional travellers to high speed rail. It therefore agrees with HS2 Ltd that such an interchange station should be included as part of the scheme put forward for public consultation, but only on the basis that an appropriate funding package is identified.

6.65 Alongside HS2 Ltd's further design work on this interchange station, the Government will work closely with the surrounding local authorities and wider West Midlands partners and businesses to ensure that all possible synergies with other development plans are fully realised, that proposals are sensitive to local requirements, and that an equitable funding package is devised.

The Government's Assessment

6.66 Subject to completion of the additional work described in this Chapter, the Government's preliminary assessment is that HS2 Ltd's recommended route, which would run from a rebuilt Euston station in London to a new Birmingham city centre station at Curzon/Fazeley Street, is viable.

6.67 On this basis, the Government has concluded that formal public consultation on the recommended route should begin in the autumn.

6.68 The Government and HS2 Ltd will also work with relevant local partners to develop plans and identify an appropriate funding package, including third party contributions, for each of the major station and interchange developments.

7. High Speed Two – International Connections

7.1 As a part of its work on the options for a new high speed rail line from London to the West Midlands, HS2 Ltd considered the case for providing links to Heathrow Airport and to the existing High Speed One line to the Channel Tunnel.

7.2 This Chapter sets out HS2 Ltd's recommendations in each case, and the Government's response, including the further work that it considers necessary in the light of HS2 Ltd's findings.

Connections to Heathrow Airport

7.3 In conjunction with High Speed Two, a new Crossrail Interchange station would transform connectivity to Heathrow for rail passengers from the Midlands and the North.

7.4 At present, passengers arriving at Euston, Kings Cross and St Pancras face either a journey of an hour or more to Heathrow on the Piccadilly Line, or an Underground journey to Paddington (especially inconvenient from Euston, where passengers must leave the station and cross a busy road junction to get to Euston Square Underground station), from where they can take the Heathrow Express, taking up to an hour in total. By contrast, the Crossrail Interchange station would provide a quick and convenient connection onto the Heathrow Express, with a journey time of approximately ten minutes to the airport.

7.5 In addition to, or instead of, a Crossrail Interchange, a strategic case has been advanced for a direct rail link to Heathrow to be provided as part of any high speed line from London to the West Midlands. HS2 Ltd therefore also looked at a range of options for an at-airport high speed rail station. Its analysis clearly demonstrated the significant difficulties associated with such a station. The dispersed nature of Heathrow's terminal facilities means that there is no clearly optimal location for a high speed rail station which would enable travellers to quickly access their flight, whatever terminal it left from. Both Terminal 4 and Terminal 5 are a significant distance from the current Central Terminal Area, as would be the proposed Terminal 6. Figure 7.1 demonstrates this.

High Speed Two – International Connections

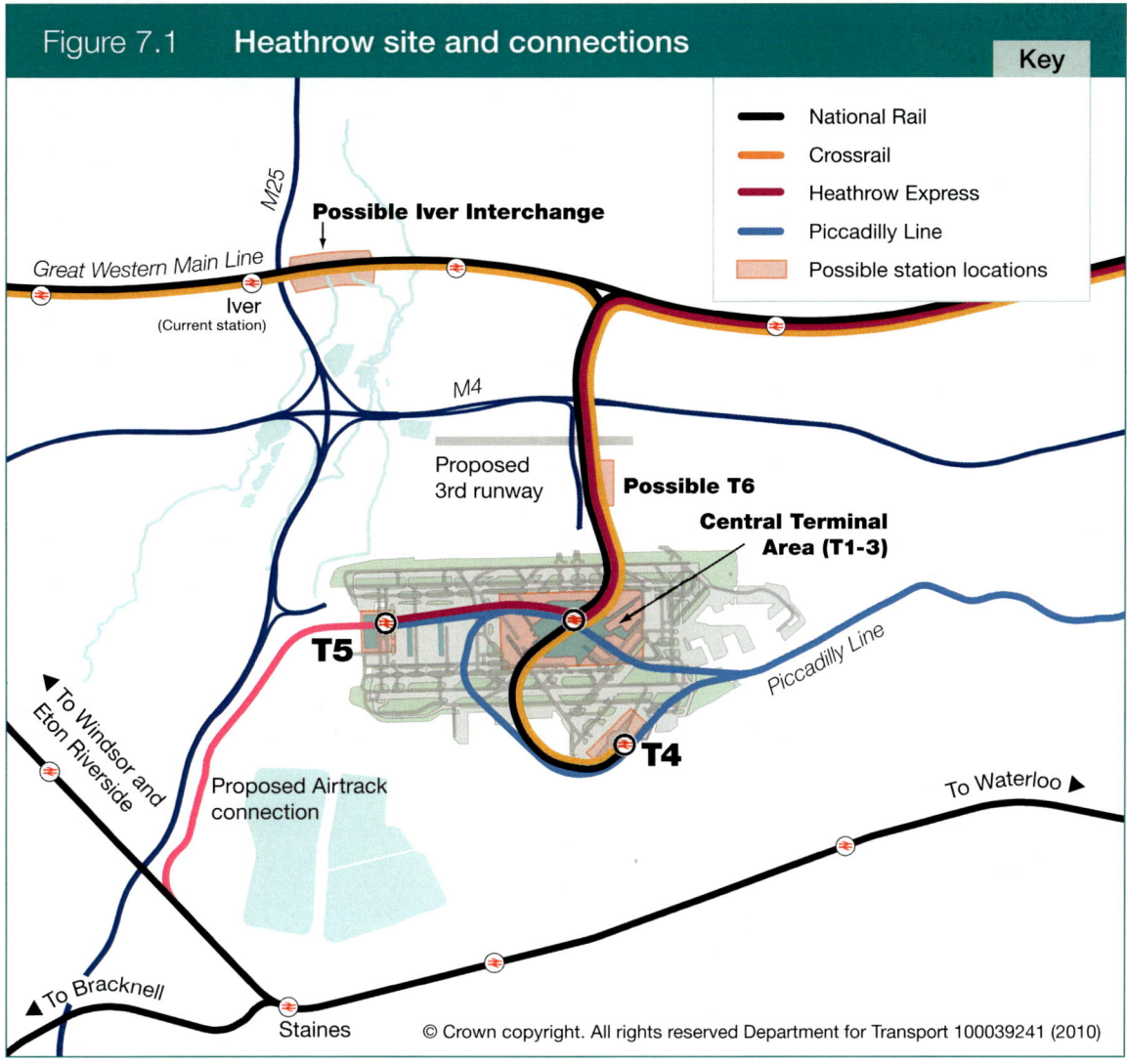

Figure 7.1 Heathrow site and connections

7.6 A proposal has been made, which HS2 Ltd considered, for a station outside the current airport boundary at Iver. This could provide good links to existing transport networks including the Great Western Main Line and the M4 and M25 motorways. But it is at some distance from the airport (about 2.5 miles from the current boundary) and divided from it by a heavily built-up area.

7.7 HS2 Ltd's analysis also indicates that there is no credible route for a high speed line to the airport – either as part of the main line, or as a loop or spur – which would not pass mainly through residential areas, and would therefore require significant and expensive tunnelling. The only credible option for routing the main high speed line via Heathrow would entail a near-continuous tunnel of around 29 miles – almost the length of the Channel Tunnel – as well as increasing the journey time by around three and a half minutes compared to HS2 Ltd's recommended route. Even if only a spur to the airport was provided, which would substantially reduce the capacity of the line to central London as Heathrow trains would terminate at the airport, the tunnelling required would lead to costs in excess of £1.5 billion.

7.8 Given the complexity and high cost of serving an at-airport station at Heathrow, and the availability of rapid and convenient connections for High Speed Two passengers via the Crossrail Interchange station, it is vital to carefully evaluate the market in considering the case for such a link.

7.9 In the case of the passengers who are perhaps most likely to transfer to high speed rail from air – those who currently travel to London by air from UK regional airports – the decision to transfer to high speed rail will not be influenced by how High Speed Two serves Heathrow. These passengers' interests will be best served by a high speed route which provides the fastest transit time and most convenient connections to the capital itself.

7.10 HS2 Ltd's analysis identifies three further markets which might be more likely to make use of an at-airport station at Heathrow. These are considered below:

- Passengers currently travelling to Heathrow by car and other surface access modes. This market is large, with around 40 million journeys per year made in total; however, only around 2.5 million of these originate in the regions most effectively served by High Speed Two (the West Midlands, the North West and beyond) and only a small percentage of those can realistically be expected to transfer to High Speed Two given their diverse starting points.

- Passengers who currently fly from regional airports to Heathrow in order to transfer to long haul flights. This market is much smaller than the surface access market, for instance just 2 million journeys per year in total from Manchester, Newcastle, Glasgow and Edinburgh airports, although this is expected to double over the next 20 years. Moreover, it is not obvious that a significant proportion of these travellers would transfer to high speed rail unless some specific challenges could be addressed – in particular, the convenience for air passengers of checking in luggage all the way to their final destination, the risk of missed connections, and the economic incentives for airlines with significant 'feeder' networks to keep fares low in order to maintain their competitive advantage.

- Passengers who currently fly from UK regional airports to European hub airports, such as Amsterdam, to connect with long haul flights. Each year some four million passengers make such flights from Birmingham, Manchester, Glasgow and Edinburgh and other airports. Whilst there may be scope for some of these to transfer to high speed rail, especially given the wide range of long haul destinations served by Heathrow, the same challenges as described above would still apply.

7.11 This analysis suggests that the current market for access to Heathrow via an at-airport high speed rail station is comparatively modest – as few as 2,000 passengers per day, according to HS2 Ltd's modelling. Such a station could be used by other passengers to reach destinations to the west of London, particularly if it provided convenient connections to Crossrail, the London Underground and the Great Western Main Line.

High Speed Two – International Connections

7.12 The vast majority of those passengers' interests would also be served by the proposed Crossrail Interchange station, however, as Table 7.1 indicates. Even in relation to passengers who would use an at-airport station to access Heathrow itself, HS2 Ltd's modelling suggests that nearly three quarters would still travel by High Speed Two if access was provided via a direct link to the Heathrow Express at its recommended Crossrail Interchange station.

Table 7.1 Forecast Distribution of HS2 Passengers Per Day

	With No Interchange station	With Crossrail Interchange station	With Heathrow at-airport station
Forecast users of second London station by final destination			
Greater London		31200	13800
Heathrow		1400	2000
Other		17400	24400
Total		50000	40200
Forecast users of Euston by final destination			
Greater London	113200	84000	79200
Heathrow	1000	0	0
Other	20000	11000	9200
Total	134200	94800	88400
Total HS2 passengers to London	**134200**	**144800**	**128600**

7.13 Given the limited size of the market for an at-airport station at Heathrow, HS2 Ltd's analysis also takes into account the potential disbenefits for the large majority of High Speed Two travellers making inter-urban journeys in considering the case for a direct link.

7.14 The disbenefits of routing the main High Speed Two line via Heathrow would be substantial, increasing journey times for non-airport passengers by around three and a half minutes because of the longer approach to central London, and the fact that trains would otherwise be travelling at full speed at the same distance from London if a more direct alignment was used. For this reason, combined with the very substantial additional costs involved of over £3 billion compared to the recommended route, HS2 Ltd did not recommend serving Heathrow in this way.

7.15 HS2 Ltd also identified significant disbenefits for inter-urban travellers from the spur and loop options. The cheapest option, a spur, would considerably reduce capacity into central London by diverting a number of services to terminate at Heathrow. A station on a loop from the main high speed line was therefore considered by HS2 Ltd to be the best option. It could combine faster direct services to the West Midlands with slower services via Heathrow, thereby limiting the impact on passengers not wishing to access the airport. Nonetheless, HS2 Ltd's analysis suggested that the demand for Heathrow services would not justify either the costs of a loop to the airport (which it estimated as between £3.1 billion and £3.6 billion depending on the station location) or the longer journey times for many inter-urban passengers.

7.16 The Government has considered HS2 Ltd's findings regarding the options and market for a high speed link to an at-airport station at Heathrow. It agrees with HS2 Ltd that the current market for such services would be low, and that any option would entail significant cost and journey time or capacity disbenefits for other travellers. It also notes the lack of a credible option for such a station which could efficiently serve all of Heathrow's existing terminals, even before its future expansion is taken into account. The Government therefore accepts HS2 Ltd's recommendation that the option put forward for public consultation should be to provide a rail link to Heathrow via the direct connection to the Heathrow Express at the Crossrail Interchange.

7.17 Nonetheless, the Government also believes that the importance of effective integration between national and international transport networks is only likely to grow stronger in the light of increasing globalisation and tighter constraints on carbon emissions. As a result, the economic and social value of a direct high speed link to Heathrow may rise, and the possibility of the potential market growing rapidly should not be ruled out, particularly given the Government's proposal for a core network reaching to Manchester and Leeds and offering significant journey time savings to other destinations including Edinburgh and Glasgow.

7.18 For these reasons, the Government's view is that, as foreshadowed in paragraph 57 of the Government's 2009 Decision on Adding Capacity at Heathrow, further assessment is needed of the case for a potential station at Heathrow Airport itself. The Government has appointed Lord Mawhinney to assess the options, and their respective business cases, taking account of the work published by HS2 Ltd, the study already underway by the airport operator, and the proposals that have been put forward for a station at Iver.

Connections to High Speed One and the Channel Tunnel

7.19 A connection from High Speed Two via the existing High Speed One line to the Channel Tunnel would provide a direct link to the European high speed rail network and allow direct services to run between major British and

European cities. The journey to Paris from Birmingham could take as little as three hours 15 minutes, and from Manchester around four hours, potentially fast enough to influence passengers to switch from air to rail.

7.20 The strategic case for a High Speed Two/High Speed One link is obvious, and the Government has asked HS2 Ltd to develop proposals for such a link, in the context of the analysis below.

7.21 According to HS2 Ltd's analysis, the initial market for high speed rail journeys from major regional cities to the Continent would be relatively small, even allowing for the expected growth in demand for long distance travel. Table 7.2 shows the total forecast annual passenger demand for journeys by air to and from Birmingham and Manchester in 2033. In the case of journeys between Birmingham and Paris, this level of demand would be equivalent to some 600 passengers per day flying in each direction.

Table 7.2 Air passenger numbers to/from Birmingham and Manchester

Total annual air passengers 2033 (thousands)	Paris CDG	Brussels	Amsterdam
Birmingham	439	284	432
Manchester	880	308	589

7.22 It is also estimated that annual rail travel between Birmingham and Paris is forecast to grow to around 130,000 by 2033.

7.23 Given that not all travellers would transfer to rail, HS2 Ltd's assessment is that direct high speed services between Birmingham and Paris/Brussels could attract around half of the combined rail/air market with some 600 to 1250 daily passengers to and from Paris and 450 to 950 daily passengers to and from Brussels. Lower proportions of air passengers would be expected to switch to rail from Manchester and other cities where rail journey times would be less competitive.

7.24 When considered in the context of the large capacity of high speed trains – up to 1100 seats per train – these predicted passenger numbers suggest that the market would be unlikely to justify running a large number of direct European services until a larger market develops.

7.25 Although the proposed route of High Speed Two in North London is relatively close to that of High Speed One, creating a physical connection between the two routes in such a heavily built up area is complex. HS2 Ltd's work indicates that a direct high speed connection to High Speed One would be prohibitively expensive, requiring a dedicated tunnel from Old Oak Common to the Barking area and costing some £3.5 billion. For this reason, HS2 Ltd has identified an alternative option for a link using the conventional rail network in North London and connecting with High Speed One near St Pancras. This would still require some tunnelling and other major track works, but would be very significantly cheaper than the high speed option, with an estimated cost of around £0.5 billion (excluding risk and ancillary costs).

7.26 In both cases, if a link between High Speed One and High Speed Two does form part of longer-term plans, then to avoid significant disruption to High Speed Two services after commencement, HS2 Ltd recommend that a direct rail link between High Speed Two and High Speed One should be built at the same time as High Speed Two.

7.27 Given the high costs of a direct rail link between High Speed One and High Speed Two, HS2 Ltd also considered improving connections for passengers between Euston and St Pancras International stations, not only to provide an efficient link between high speed rail lines, but also to improve access to conventional rail and London Underground services and to ease dispersal at Euston. As an alternative option to a direct rail link, HS2 Ltd's report considered that a dedicated rapid transit system between the two stations and running parallel to the Euston Road could provide an effective way of achieving this.

7.28 In light of the potential for future demand for connections between European high speed rail services and any domestic high speed line, but given that more work is needed to confirm whether there is a viable economic case for a link, the Government has asked HS2 Ltd to further develop options for both a direct rail link to High Speed One via the existing North London network and an improved passenger connection between Euston and St Pancras, to include detailed assessments of their respective business cases.

8. Design Standards and Regulation

8.1 Alongside its work on the route, stations and international connections of a London-Birmingham high speed line, HS2 Ltd also considered a number of issues relating to the technical specification of High Speed Two. This included consideration of the rolling stock that would use such a line, and the potential options for use of the line and of released capacity elsewhere on the network by long-distance, commuter and freight services. It also considered the future options for regulation.

8.2 This Chapter presents HS2 Ltd's recommendations in each case, and the Government's response, including the further work that it considers necessary in the light of HS2 Ltd's findings.

Technical Specification – Route Design

8.3 The Government agrees with HS2 Ltd's decision to design High Speed Two to provide for an ultimate maximum speed of 250 miles per hour, with a view to accommodating train service speeds of 225 miles per hour, in line with current best practice. The Government recognises and accepts that this necessarily constrains the maximum acceptable track curvature and gradients, which in turn restricts the number of potential route options. For example, as Chapter Six sets out, it would not be possible for the new line closely to follow the route of the M1 or M40. The Government considers that HS2 Ltd has recommended a potentially viable route which can accommodate an ultimate maximum speed of 250 miles per hour on route sections where train performance or other factors such as environmental considerations permit.

8.4 HS2 Ltd's technical specification for High Speed Two complies fully with EU Technical Specifications for Interoperability (TSI), including European structure gauge. The Government agrees with this approach, which accords with its policy of future-proofing the rail system by building new rail infrastructure in accordance with the TSIs and, where appropriate, progressively upgrading the existing rail infrastructure in line with these.

Rolling Stock

8.5 HS2 Ltd's report notes that compliance with European TSIs will permit the use of European rolling stock on High Speed Two and allow for the possibility of through-running between the European rail network and the new line – for instance, by requiring infrastructure, and in particular station platforms, to be designed to accommodate two 200-metre long trains, separately or coupled to run together. Both the Channel Tunnel and High Speed One, the high speed link into London, are already constructed to European loading gauge.

8.6 HS2 Ltd therefore proposes that the rolling stock fleet which would operate solely on High Speed Two should be built to take advantage of the larger clearances. This will allow these new trains to be more spacious – taller and wider – than any of Britain's existing rolling stock, and will permit the use of existing international standard high speed train designs. The Government agrees with this recommendation.

8.7 The Government also notes that such European standard rolling stock would not be able to run onto the current British rail network, and that HS2 Ltd's analysis suggests that the full benefits of the initial High Speed Two route, or indeed of a wider high speed network, would only be realised if through-services via existing tracks are provided to destinations beyond the reach of the high speed lines.

The latest in European high speed train design – the French AGV

Design Standards and Regulation

8.8 HS2 Ltd's report identifies two options for providing such services: either through the use of 'classic-compatible' high speed trains built to the smaller UK loading gauge, or through gauge clearing the sections of the existing network needed to enable European-sized high speed trains to run on it to reach their final destinations. Gauge clearance would mean significant alterations to the track and to structures such as bridges, tunnels and stations to allow the passage of wider and higher trains. Such major works could be costly and widely disruptive to existing train services.

8.9 The Government accepts that procuring classic-compatible high speed trains will be more expensive than international standard designs built to the European loading gauge, but it agrees with HS2 Ltd that it is still likely to be considerably more cost effective to provide a classic-compatible fleet of trains rather than undertake large-scale gauge clearance work on the existing network. A classic-compatible fleet is also a more flexible solution.

8.10 The Government is therefore minded to endorse HS2 Ltd's recommendation of a mixed fleet of dedicated and classic-compatible high speed trains for High Speed Two. In the first instance, the dedicated trains would provide services only between London and Birmingham, while the classic-compatible trains would be used for through services to destinations beyond Birmingham.

8.11 However, given that HS2 Ltd's assessment of the balance of advantage was based only on the High Speed Two line to the West Midlands and not on the extended 'Y' network, the Government has asked the company for advice on whether this conclusion, and the recommended mix of dedicated and classic compatible trains, still holds for the 'Y' network, albeit with a much greater number of dedicated high speed trains.

8.12 Over the longer term, should Britain's high speed network be extended, there would be increasing scope for services to be provided by the more spacious and dedicated high speed trains possibly including double-deck rolling stock. The classic-compatible trains will continue to perform a valuable role, however, by being reassigned to operate new services extending the benefits of the high speed network beyond its expanded limits.

8.13 The Government accepts that it is not generally appropriate for existing non-high speed rolling stock to use the new high speed line as its inferior operating characteristics would consume several high speed train paths, and prevent optimum usage of the new high speed line.

8.14 The Government endorses HS2 Ltd's recommendation that both dedicated and classic-compatible rolling stock sets should have consistent operating characteristics, with distributed traction and a maximum speed in both cases of at least 225 miles per hour (360 kilometres per hour).

8.15 The Government also accepts HS2 Ltd's recommendation that the dedicated fleet should be configured as 200-metre sets, to run singly or in pairs according to demand requirements. The Government acknowledges that stations on the current network will generally only be able to accommodate 200-metre sets.

Maintenance and Stabling Depots

8.16 HS2 Ltd noted that High Speed Two would require a rolling stock depot, a principal infrastructure maintenance depot and subsidiary depots at key points along the route. It would also require various other equipment locations including London terminal stabling, a control centre and power supply facilities. For the rolling stock and maintenance depots, HS2 Ltd identified four factors which need to be considered in assessing potential site suitability: location; site requirements; access to relevant rail routes; and sustainability criteria.

8.17 HS2 Ltd assumed that a single depot would maintain both the dedicated and classic-compatible fleets and that it should be located in the West Midlands. As well as effectively serving the High Speed Two line, this would be roughly at the mid-point of the wider network extending to Manchester and Leeds. A site in the Washwood Heath area of Birmingham was regarded as a credible option for more detailed assessment, although HS2 Ltd recommended that further consideration also be given to alternatives.

8.18 For the principal infrastructure maintenance depot, a location adjacent to the crossing of the Bletchley-Oxford line was identified as a potential option, by virtue of the classic rail connectivity this would provide, but again, further work is required.

8.19 The Government agrees with HS2 Ltd that the West Midlands could be an appropriate location for a rolling stock depot, including for its proposed wider 'Y' network, and has asked HS2 Ltd to do further work on this and on the other depots and related facilities in time to inform a formal public consultation in the autumn. Final decisions should be taken following consultation if and when a preferred line of route is confirmed.

Freight

8.20 HS2 Ltd found that the additional costs of making High Speed Two capable of carrying freight would be negligible (compliance with European TSIs means that High Speed Two would be capable of accepting European gauge wagons). The Government agrees that this could be important in providing for high speed international rail-freight services, in competition with air freight, as well as enhancing overall network resilience.

8.21 However, the Government concurs with HS2 Ltd's conclusion that it would not be feasible to permit conventional freight services (or other slower trains) onto High Speed Two as part of its normal operations, because of their severe impact on line capacity.

8.22 The more significant benefit for the UK rail freight industry and its customers from High Speed Two would lie in the capacity a new line would release to support continued growth in freight operations on the West Coast Main Line and other existing routes.

Design Standards and Regulation

8.23 The West Coast Main Line is Britain's key trunk route for rail-borne freight, with around half of UK rail freight using it during some part of its journey. It forms a vital international trade link between the major gateway ports of the South East and the conurbations of the Midlands, North West and Scotland, as well as serving key freight interchanges in the West Midlands and North West. However, the West Coast Main Line is also currently operating very near to line capacity, with little opportunity for freight operators to secure additional freight paths.

8.24 This capacity constraint acts as a brake on the modal shift of freight from road to rail. The use for freight purposes of some of the additional capacity on the West Coast Main Line that would be released as a result of High Speed Two could make an important contribution to addressing this.

8.25 The service specification modelled by HS2 Ltd to inform the business case for High Speed Two assumes a notional distribution of released capacity between freight, regional and commuter passenger services. However, the Government recognises that the actual allocation of capacity would be carried out through industry processes, and it would look to facilitate freight use of such capacity where appropriate through related investment in the capacity and capability of the Strategic Freight Network.

Regulation

8.26 High Speed Two would require an effective system of regulation. The particular nature of this regulatory system would depend on a number of factors, most notably the structure put in place for the operation of services on the line. For instance, the number of potential train operators using High Speed Two, including the scope for open access services, would have implications for the scale of the regulator's task.

8.27 The goals of the regulatory structure for High Speed Two would be likely to encompass:

- ensuring that the line is operated in accordance with best practice in safeguarding passenger and workforce safety;
- ensuring that the line is operated in a manner that provides value for money for funders (including the taxpayer);
- requiring the infrastructure operator to manage the asset and to behave in an efficient and effective manner; and
- meeting EU regulatory requirements.

8.28 Should there be a requirement to regulate access rights to the line, the regulator would be required to determine the appropriate level of access charges to be paid by train service operators, and to establish structures for deciding upon access rights.

8.29 The existing rail network in Britain is regulated by the Office of Rail Regulation (ORR), which acts as a combined safety and economic regulator. The obvious course, in terms of efficiency and the sharing of expertise, would be to extend the ORR's remit to cover High Speed Two. The ORR is already accustomed to setting track access charges, determining access rights and ensuring that Network Rail, the owner and operator of the existing rail network, makes continuing improvements to safety and efficiency. It also undertakes analogous functions in respect of the High Speed One link to the Channel Tunnel, operated by HS1 Ltd.

8.30 However, at this stage, the Government does not believe that any option should be ruled out, ranging from the ORR regulating High Speed Two to a new high speed rail regulatory structure being put in place with dedicated responsibility for any high speed network.

8.31 There may also be further questions relating to the nature of the regulator's interface with the public. Although it has wide ranging duties, including protecting the interests of railway users, the ORR is perceived as an industry-facing body, with Passenger Focus having primary responsibility for responding to and promoting the concerns of passengers. The Government would want to consider the appropriate mechanisms for ensuring that the concerns of passengers using High Speed Two (and any future wider network) are represented adequately.

Role of Network Rail

8.32 Network Rail will have a key role to play as HS2 Ltd develops its proposals for a new high speed line to the West Midlands and potentially beyond. The company owns and operates infrastructure which would be central to those proposals, notably Euston station and operational railway land at Old Oak Common and the Chiltern Line. Furthermore, all options for a new line, including HS2 Ltd's recommended route, would require new high speed rolling stock to operate not just on the new line but on the conventional network, where their timetables would need to mesh with those of conventional services.

8.33 The Government and HS2 Ltd will therefore work closely with Network Rail prior to consultation on both the further development of HS2 Ltd's recommendations and the broader strategy for high speed rail. This is without prejudice to future decisions on where responsibility for the construction, ownership, operation and maintenance of any new high speed line should rest.

Part 3: The Way Forward

St Pancras Station, restored, expanded and reopened in 2007 as the terminus for High Speed One.

9. Engagement and Consultation

9.1 In Part Two of this Command Paper, the Government set out its response to the detailed proposal developed by HS2 Ltd for a high speed line from London to the West Midlands, which would provide the foundation for a core high speed rail network. On the basis of the evidence provided, the Government's assessment is that HS2 Ltd's recommended route is viable, subject to further work being completed to mitigate a number of specific environmental impacts.

9.2 Part Three sets out the Government's plan for taking forward the work that HS2 Ltd has undertaken to date and for developing a wider strategy for high speed rail. Of fundamental importance within this process will be formal public consultation on the detail of HS2 Ltd's recommended route option from London to Birmingham, and on the Government's strategic proposals for high speed rail. A consultation 'routemap' is provided later in this chapter. The subsequent chapters deal with what would be entailed in securing the powers to allow such a route to be constructed, and an outline of the likely key elements and timing of the construction process itself.

9.3 The Government is mindful of the need for ongoing engagement with stakeholders even ahead of formal public consultation. This process of pre-consultation is important to ensure that the formal public consultation is communicated successfully to interested parties and particularly those most likely to be affected by HS2 Ltd's recommendations. It will also help to ensure that proposed activities to raise awareness of the consultation are taken forward on an informed basis and are configured such that all interested parties have access to the consultation materials and have an opportunity to comment.

9.4 This chapter sets out the public engagement activities that the Government and HS2 Ltd will now take forward to inform the Government's preparation of the formal public consultation planned for the autumn. These activities will build on the stakeholder engagement which HS2 Ltd undertook in 2009 to inform its report to Government.

Dealing with uncertainty and blight

9.5 Under existing planning law, residential and agricultural owner occupiers directly affected by any confirmed plans for the development of any future high speed line would have access in due course to statutory blight provisions, which would apply from such time as safeguarding directions are issued in respect of any route. These provisions also apply to commercial properties with an annual rateable value of no more than £29,000.

9.6 The possibility of such a line being constructed, however, may in some cases have an impact on property values in the period before statutory protection is available. There is no statutory remedy for this, but the Government accepts that those most affected by HS2 Ltd's recommendations for a London-Birmingham high speed line should have access to redress.

9.7 The Government therefore proposes to introduce an Exceptional Hardship Scheme for householders most affected by these recommendations, and in particular for householders who have an urgent need to relocate. It is intended first to consult on this and, alongside this Command Paper, the Government has published a consultation paper setting out its proposals on the scope of such a scheme. This consultation paper is available on the Department for Transport website at: www.dft.gov.uk/consultations/open/

9.8 The consultation period will run until 20 May 2010, with a view to launching the scheme shortly thereafter.

Public Information

9.9 The Department for Transport will maintain a full selection of the relevant documentation on its website, allowing interested parties to gain ready access to the information they require on high speed rail. These documents can be accessed at www.dft.gov.uk/highspeedrail

9.10 The Department has also prepared a CD-ROM containing all of the relevant documents, including HS2 Ltd's report and supporting material as well as this Command Paper. These CD-ROMs can be ordered free of charge from DfT Publications.[8] Printed copies of this Command Paper can be ordered from The Stationery Office.

9.11 The Government will operate an enquiry line to address questions relating not only to blight and the consultation, but also wider questions about both HS2 Ltd's work to date and the Government's proposed strategy on high speed rail as set out in this document. The enquiry line will act as a ready portal for all interested parties to gain information. It is not, however, intended as a substitute for formal public consultation, which is to follow in due course.

9.12 The enquiry line can be contacted on 020 7944 4908.

---

8 See http://www.dft.gov.uk/foi/dftps/howtoobtaindftpublications or tel: 0300 123 1102

Stakeholder Engagement

9.13 HS2 Ltd's consultation strategy, submitted to the Government alongside its main report, advised that engaging stakeholders at an early stage ahead of the launch of the formal public consultation would be beneficial in a number of respects. The Government recognises the importance of continuing the work that HS2 Ltd has already started.

9.14 This pre-consultation engagement does not preclude the need for formal public consultation, but simply ensures that such consultation is as effective as possible. The Government will work alongside HS2 Ltd in continuing this engagement with key stakeholders.

9.15 Engagement at this stage will help to ensure that any particular local, regional or cultural sensitivities are fully factored into consultation and communication plans and, therefore, that the formal public consultation process planned for the autumn enables all interested parties to register their views. We expect this engagement also to involve representative groups with strong potential interests in the proposals for high speed rail and their impacts. Advice from these groups will be important in ensuring that communications activities are conducted in the most effective way possible.

9.16 A wide range of both local and national stakeholders, representing a diversity of potential interests, are likely to be keen to input to the consultation. The Government will be responsive, as far as it reasonably can be, to the different needs of these groupings, ensuring that all parties are presented with the opportunity to comment on HS2 Ltd's recommendations. The Government will work with local authorities and other representative bodies on devising appropriate public consultation strategies for their areas.

9.17 It is important that key minority groups are empowered to respond to the consultation. The Government recognises that this is likely to necessitate more extensive pre-consultation engagement, to allow an effective public consultation strategy to be devised.

9.18 The Government acknowledges HS2 Ltd's advice that these pre-consultation activities are likely to need to be conducted over a number of months – as many as six – ahead of the formal public consultation.

Formal Consultation

9.19 A project of the scope of High Speed Two has potential implications for many individuals, families, communities and businesses.

9.20 The engagement process described in this chapter will enable HS2 Ltd and the Government to understand better the concerns and interests of those potentially affected by, or interested in, any new high speed line, and it will inform the further development of both the Government's proposed strategy for high speed rail and HS2 Ltd's detailed recommendations prior to consultation. However, it is not and nor is it meant to be a substitute for formal public consultation.

9.21 The Government proposes to begin formal public consultation in the autumn, following completion of the additional work requested by the Government from HS2 Ltd on its recommended route from London to the West Midlands. This consultation will provide an opportunity for all interested parties to express their view on HS2 Ltd's recommended route and on the mitigation measures that HS2 Ltd proposes to reduce any potential adverse impacts on individuals, communities and the environment.

9.22 The consultation questions posed will be set out in detail in a formal public consultation paper. They will also include questions on strategic issues relating to the key transport challenges to be addressed, the options to consider for addressing them, the weight to be attached to various factors in assessing those options, and the strategic conclusions reached as a result. The responses to these questions will inform the Government's consideration of its proposed strategy for high speed rail.

9.23 To inform this consultation, the Government will publish alongside its consultation paper a full Appraisal of Sustainability which will take into account the conclusions of the further work that has been commissioned from HS2 Ltd, as well as detailed maps and descriptions of the proposed route.

9.24 Given the particular interests and concerns of those living and working close to the recommended route, HS2 Ltd will also hold engagement events in a number of key towns and villages, which will enable those people to pose questions about its detailed proposals and about how to respond formally to the consultation.

9.25 The Government expects to hold a similar formal public consultation in due course, but not before early 2012, on the options for the routes from Birmingham to Manchester and Leeds, following completion of HS2 Ltd's detailed planning work. This expectation may, of course, be revised in the light of the consultation later this year and HS2 Ltd's recommendations.

9.26 The Government will not make a final decision on the detailed recommendations made by HS2 Ltd or on its proposed strategy for high speed rail until it has received responses to these consultation exercises. If it decides in the light of those responses that the routes recommended are viable and that any or all of them should be taken forward, the Government will commission HS2 Ltd to begin the work needed to prepare for seeking the necessary powers via a Hybrid Bill, including environmental impact assessment, other requisite assessment processes and further appropriate public and stakeholder consultations.

10. Planning Consents and Construction

10.1 The previous chapter explained the Government's plans to consult on the initial assessments set out in this Command Paper and for an Exceptional Hardship Scheme to deal with any unavoidable generalised blight issues whilst public consultation is underway.

10.2 Following completion of those consultations, and subject to their results, if the Government concludes that a high speed rail network should form a key part of the UK's future inter-urban transport infrastructure, then it proposes to secure the necessary powers for its delivery through a single Hybrid Bill. Hybrid Bills are a tried and tested means of securing planning and legal powers for major new railway lines. Crossrail, High Speed One and the Dartford Crossing were all successfully taken forward by means of Hybrid Bills.

10.3 The Hybrid Bill process, by which the Government can promote Bills which would affect the private interests of particular people or organisations, allows those affected by a scheme to petition Parliament directly and seek amendments before the relevant Select Committees in both Houses.

10.4 However, because such a Bill is enacted as primary legislation, this process also allows the Government to seek all the necessary statutory powers and authorisations that a complex scheme such as a high speed rail network would require. These could include, amongst other things, revisions to the rail regulatory regime, public finance provisions, and provisions to enable the Secretary of State to make subsequent orders and regulations by way of a statutory instrument.

10.5 Whilst it would be possible to seek powers for each leg of any high speed rail network through separate Hybrid Bills, the Government's view is that this would not be viable in practice, and that subject to a decision to proceed, a single Hybrid Bill should encompass the core initial 'Y' network from London to Birmingham, Manchester and Leeds. The passage of a Hybrid Bill requires significant Parliamentary time and therefore any other approach would create significant uncertainty about whether and when powers for subsequent legs could be secured, which would impact upon the consideration of the initial legislation.

10.6 A second advantage to securing powers via a single Hybrid Bill is that it would enable construction of the network, should Parliamentary approval be granted, to be planned as a single coherent project. This could potentially reduce costs and bring forward completion, particularly of the later stages, as some of those works could potentially be carried out concurrently with construction of the initial route.

10.7 Therefore, if the Government remains of the view, following consultation, that the core High Speed Two network should consist of routes from London to Birmingham and on to Manchester and Leeds, it proposes to seek powers for the whole of that network through a single Hybrid Bill, and will ask HS2 Ltd to take forward the necessary planning and preparation work, including environmental impact assessment and other requisite assessments, to enable such a Bill to be introduced as and when Parliamentary business allows.

Mobilisation and Construction

10.8 If a Hybrid Bill is enacted and powers are obtained, there would be significant further work before construction of a new high speed network could begin.

10.9 HS2 Ltd estimates that this phase, referred to as mobilisation, could last around two years. This time would be required to allow for land assembly, and commencement of initial utilities diversions and temporary works, as well as to finalise the funding package for the network, carry out advanced planning of the construction phase and let contracts.

10.10 Following completion of the mobilisation phase, and once funding and construction contracts are in place, HS2 Ltd estimate that the construction of the London-Birmingham route would take around six and a half years. This timing is driven by the length of time needed to complete the most significant works, which, if HS2 Ltd's recommended route is taken forward, would be likely to be at Euston station and its approaches. Other major works, such as at Curzon/Fazeley Street in Birmingham or at the Crossrail Interchange in West London, could also take four years or more to complete.

10.11 As set out above, however, one of the key advantages of securing powers for a network through a single Hybrid Bill is that this would allow construction of different stages of the overall network to be planned in parallel. As well as reducing costs by providing additional long-term certainty to construction contractors and other supply chain firms, this could enable construction resources freed up by the completion of smaller parts of the London to Birmingham route to begin concurrent work on other parts of the network. As a result, it is likely that the network could be completed sooner than if each leg were delivered sequentially.

10.12 The final phase before passenger services could begin on any new high speed line would be a period of testing and commissioning. This period would be used to test the operation of the infrastructure and rolling stock, as well as to carry out safety checks and staff recruitment and training. Whilst this phase, which HS2 Ltd estimates as lasting around two years, could begin prior to the completion of construction, a substantial proportion would still have to take place after the entire line was built.

10.13 These estimates may be subject to significant change. Alterations to the scope of the project, for instance, as a result of consultation, would entail additional design and preparation works. And neither the duration nor the success of Parliamentary approval processes can be guaranteed. Once powers were secured, final decisions on the phasing of the project would be likely to depend on public finance considerations at the time.

10.14 Subject to public consultation, environmental impact assessment, Parliamentary approval and decisions on funding, the Government's preliminary assessment is that it should be possible for a London to Birmingham line to open by the end of 2026, with the London to Manchester routes to follow in subsequent years, subject to the same principal considerations.

11. Costs and Funding

11.1 HS2 Ltd's calculations indicate that the cost of designing and building a line from London to the West Midlands would be between £15.8 billion and £17.4 billion, including appropriate provision for risk, at 2009 prices.

11.2 Although it has not done the same level of detailed planning, and therefore a significantly higher level of uncertainty must be acknowledged, HS2 Ltd's initial assessment of the total infrastructure cost of an initial core network linking London to Birmingham, Manchester and Leeds, and connecting to the West and East Coast Main Lines close to Preston and York respectively, is in the region of £30 billion.

11.3 In both cases, there would be substantial additional costs, most notably the cost of rolling stock. HS2 Ltd estimate this would be around £3 billion for a London-West Midlands line, and considerably higher for a wider high speed network.

11.4 There would also be long-term costs associated with the ongoing operation and maintenance of any new high speed line, although HS2 Ltd's calculations suggest that these would be exceeded by the revenues generated from ticket sales and other sources.

11.5 Whilst these costs are clearly significant, they would be spread out over a period of 15 or more years and the largest sums would not begin to be spent until during construction. Furthermore, the rate of expenditure would depend significantly on decisions about the phasing of individual segments of the overall scheme.

11.6 In fact, under HS2 Ltd's proposed spend profile, the average annual expenditure during the construction period would be around £2 billion, with the highest spend in a single year totalling £3.9 billion. This is broadly consistent with planned spend during the construction period for the Crossrail project.

11.7 The estimated design and preparation costs prior to the commencement of construction, along with the costs associated with the introduction and passage of a Hybrid Bill, are very significantly lower, and would depend heavily on factors such as the duration and complexity of the preparatory work and the amount of controversy and amendments encountered.

High Speed Rail

11.8 The Government is committed to long term investment in the infrastructure needed to support the UK economy. As *Building Britain's Future* explains:

"Seizing the opportunities of the future depends on having truly nationwide, high quality business and technical infrastructure. That is why we must give priority to bringing greater focus to building and modernising our economic infrastructure in energy, water, waste, communications, as well as transport and housing."

11.9 Although significant, the profiled costs estimated by HS2 Ltd and described above are in line with this long-term commitment and with the pattern of public sector investment in major infrastructure projects over recent years, such as High Speed One, Crossrail and the Olympic Park.

11.10 Using HS2 Ltd's best case scenario, construction works on any new high speed line could not begin until after the completion of Crossrail, opening from 2017, which could present opportunities for the transfer of skills and expertise and for reducing supply chain costs by providing a predictable and long term pipeline of major infrastructure projects.

11.11 Further work needs to be done to ensure that if such a project is taken forward, it is done so in a way which presents the best possible value for money. This work, described in more detail below, will focus on two areas: firstly, the potential for the delivery costs of any new high speed line to be reduced; and secondly, on the options for funding such a new high speed line, focusing in particular on maximising potential third party contributions.

Reducing the Costs of Infrastructure Delivery

11.12 HS2 Ltd's development of a proposal for a high speed line from London to the West Midlands identified some initial evidence that delivering infrastructure in the UK is more costly than for similar projects in other countries. Work to benchmark costs of major, comparable high speed rail line projects across Europe found that the UK unit rates for civil engineering works (for example, tunnels and viaducts) for a high speed rail line could be up to double those in Europe.

11.13 There is evidence to suggest that this conclusion applies more widely than simply in the rail sector. For example, a 2009 study by The Whitehall and Industry Group for the Department for Business, Innovation and Skills concluded that productivity in engineering construction could be improved, citing project management, industrial relations, and stability in investment and regulation as key issues[9]. A 2006 study by the European Commission ranked the UK joint 11th of 13 Member States for efficiency in construction, citing procurement and skills as key issues[10].

---

9 Changing to Compete: Review of Productivity and Skills in UK Engineering Construction, The Whitehall & Industry Group, December 2009
10 Benchmarking of construction efficiency in the EU Member States (Pilot study), European Commission, March 2006

11.14 Whilst it is quite possible that civil engineering costs for High Speed Two may not be double those of other countries, even a more modest five to 10 per cent difference could save up to £1.5 billion.

11.15 The Department for Transport and Infrastructure UK (IUK) will work together to consider how and whether the cost of relevant civil engineering works could be lowered, taking into account HS2 Ltd's evidence. HS2 Ltd will engage closely with IUK as this work progresses, and its cost estimates for its recommended route from London to the West Midlands will be kept under review in the light of the results emerging from this work and subsequent actions, as will the estimated costings developed in due course for the Leeds or Manchester legs.

The Funding of High Speed Two

11.16 HS2 Ltd's report considers the funding options for any potential new high speed line and concludes that a largely public sector funding approach for the upfront capital costs is likely to offer the best value for money, particularly in respect of the railway components of the project.

11.17 Alongside this, however, it also identifies a wide range of ways in which contributions to the costs of the project could be sought from non-Government funders. These might include contributions from financial and economic beneficiaries of the projects, including businesses and others in the cities that it would serve, or from other public sector sources, such as local authorities, Regional Development Agencies or the EU.

11.18 The Government agrees with these conclusions, and is determined to ensure that a fair balance should be struck in terms of the contributions made by all of those who would benefit from any new high speed network. It will therefore be reviewing further the funding options for any high speed rail network in the UK, taking particular account of the scope for securing third party contributions towards the cost of constructing such a network. These may include developer contributions linked to new station and interchange sites, and local authority funding where the project supports local economic growth. This review should also consider whether PPP structures could provide a value for money means of financing parts of any high speed rail project, for example, for rolling stock.

12. New Industry, New Jobs

12.1 A new high speed line for Britain could be seen both as a transport project and as a transformational investment underpinning Government objectives on economic growth and support for industry.

12.2 Chapters 2 and 3 outlined how high speed rail could support UK economic growth and prosperity. A long-term programme of investment in high speed rail would also present new opportunities for British design, engineering, training and development throughout the rail industry supply chain.

12.3 The Government has engaged with the key rail industry stakeholders, including the Railway Industry Association, Rail Alliance and the Regional Development Agencies on potential business opportunities associated with new high speed rail investment.

12.4 This chapter outlines the case for an active role for Government, working in partnership with industry, to ensure the UK has a supply chain that offers best value for money as well as the skills and capacity to compete and win new business, if, following public consultation, a decision is made to take High Speed Two forward.

Investing in Business Success

12.5 In April 2009 the Government launched *New Industry, New Jobs*[11] – an active industrial strategy for Britain. This sets out a strategy to equip the country to succeed over the next decade.

12.6 *Going for Growth: Our Future Prosperity*[12], published in January 2010, describes the capabilities the UK needs to invest in, and sets out a plan to achieve sustainable economic growth. High Speed Two would support this vision by providing new infrastructure to improve the overall business environment, supporting the UK's growing capability as a leader in low-carbon transport, and generating new business opportunities arising from new rail investment.

---

11 http://www.bis.gov.uk/policies/new-industry-new-jobs
12 http://www.bis.gov.uk/growth/going-for-growth

New Industry, New Jobs

The UK Supply Chain

12.7 The UK was the global pioneer of rail in the nineteenth and early-to-mid twentieth centuries. In 1910, some 800,000 people worked on the railways and the country boasted twenty five major railway works facilities, the largest (Swindon) employing 11,700 staff. In 1913 alone, 453 new steam locomotives, 931 carriages and some 50,000 wagons were built in British factories. As one railway historian has noted: "The railways were vast engineering and manufacturing businesses, quite apart from the day to day activity of moving people."[13]

12.8 In the last 30 years the rail industry has become increasingly globalised, with complex and inter-dependent supply chains that cross borders. Whilst leading to decline in some areas of UK manufacturing, this new global competition has also driven innovation and new inward investment. Today, the UK rail industry is globally competitive, estimated to employ around 190,000 people and worth at least £9 billion annually.

12.9 Competitive pressure has also led to the development of important links with the civil engineering and construction sectors, and innovative solutions developed by the rail technology base can also be used by the aerospace and automotive industries. This means that the skills developed in UK universities and businesses can transfer to other sectors and help foster innovative and green solutions in a variety of contexts.

12.10 High speed rail in Britain would present a new opportunity to develop and demonstrate ingenuity and entrepreneurial excellence. HS2 Ltd estimates that construction and operation alone of a new London-Birmingham line would directly create over 10,000 new jobs. It would also support new

---

13 M. A-C Horne, A Century of Change, Railway Studies Association, 2010

supply chain opportunities and provide a show case for world-class expertise in design, consultancy and civil engineering.

12.11 The potential value to the UK could be even greater. Chapter Three articulates the broader economic and employment benefits that high speed rail could bring to the UK, and Chapter Four outlines the Government's long-term proposal for a core British high speed rail network extending to Manchester and Leeds with through services running beyond. Should a new high speed network be developed, it could provide employment in rail services and rail freight, manufacturing, and maintenance, for decades to come.

> UK company **Pandrol** is the global market leader in rail-fastening manufacture and design, supplying innovative, good value and high-quality solutions. The French track authority Réseau Ferré de France (RFF) now uses the Pandrol FASTCLIP system on all concrete sleeper renewals and new line construction projects in France, including the construction of the new TGV Est high speed line

12.12 High Speed Two would build on the UK's existing rail industry capability, particularly in long-life, high-quality components and products. The long-term nature of the project would provide opportunities to develop a strategic plan and facilitate investment in new areas applicable to high speed rail technology where the UK does not currently have core capability and expertise, and where there is potential value to the UK. This would support a growing export market.

12.13 To support the UK's reputation as an open and competitive market, this would mean working with investors and suppliers across the globe as well as fostering close partnership with the UK supply chain.

12.14 High speed rail would capitalise on and reinforce the skills and supply chains developed through existing rail and infrastructure investment programmes. The Government has already committed to the £16 billion Crossrail project, a £5.5 billion investment in Thameslink, a major £1.3 billion programme of electrification, and wider rail modernisation and rolling stock investment. There may be potential for synergies in areas such as skills development, as well as opportunities to maximise value for money.

An Active Role for Government

12.15 The Government's early engagement with the industry has made clear that, should High Speed Two go ahead, the Government needs to start working now to secure a strong and competitive supply chain capable of delivering and supporting new business opportunities. This would require an active role for Government.

12.16 Should proposals for High Speed Two be taken forward, the Government will work with the industry to draw up a high speed rail industrial strategy. The Government envisages that this could include:

- identifying practical measures to ensure that the UK has the skills and capability to design, build and operate high speed lines;
- working with the supply chain to enable companies to plan ahead and so offer best value solutions; and
- ensuring that the way high speed rail is procured works for industry and Government alike.

12.17 To take this work forward, the Government intends, subject to consultation with industry, to establish a high level supply chain forum which would focus on the opportunities presented by high speed rail and provide advice to Ministers.

12.18 The Government will also consider:

- inviting a supply chain forum to provide industry input into the Value for Money in Rail Study and work on the unit cost of high speed rail; and
- establishing an exchange of secondees between Government and the rail industry.

12.19 Should proposals for High Speed Two be taken forward, the Government would consult on a procurement approach that supports the Rail Sustainable Procurement principles including best value for money, whole-life costs, low-carbon and sustainable employment goals, and new business opportunities in a globally competitive and open market.

> **Advantage West Midlands (AWM)**, the Regional Development Agency for the West Midlands, has set up a programme of supply-chain groupings, including for rail, bringing together groups of companies to collaborate on quality, technology and performance issues. This is leading to the development of best-practice principles throughout the supply chain.
>
> The AWM model uses complementary, existing support mechanisms to focus industry capability on new business opportunities. These mechanisms include information-sharing, technology support in conjunction with universities and research institutions, and business performance improvement by linking with 'Solutions for Business' support. This approach has helped companies develop new products and services with UK supply chains.

Supporting World-Class Skills

12.20 Investment in high speed rail would provide an opportunity to create new skilled jobs and support upskilling at every level. Skills are important not only for the delivery of a better, more efficient railway in Britain, but also in helping British industry to compete internationally.

High Speed Rail

> **Creactive Design**, a Midlands based design consultancy, has developed a new air cooling unit called Cabcool. The cooling system has been designed for drivers of trains that previously had no air conditioning or cooling system. The product is 30 per cent of the cost of installing a typical air conditioning unit and because of its innovative design it uses only 10 per cent of the energy of a typical air conditioning unit. It allows the drivers to operate in a space that was not designed with air conditioning in mind. The product has been designed and wholly manufactured in the UK and is now fitted on Victoria and Circle Line trains on the London Underground. The company is focussing on exporting the product to Northern Europe and South America.

12.21 The benefits would not be limited to the rail sector. Many of the skills and resources needed to develop high speed rail are generic to manufacturing, engineering and construction. Consequently, the UK manufacturing and construction sectors, and especially civil engineering, could be expected to benefit more generally.

12.22 The Government has laid out its strategy to meet the skills needs of the future in *Skills for Growth*[14], published in November 2009, and *Higher Ambitions*[15], the strategy for higher education. Key measures include widening of access to higher education through apprenticeship and vocational routes, with more flexible and workplace-based courses. There will be enhanced support for science, technology, engineering and mathematics subjects: key skill sets required by the next generation of rail engineers, apprentices and technicians.

12.23 A bid to the Learning and Skills Council for a new National Skills Academy for Rail Engineering has been submitted and shortlisted. This will help to ensure that the engineering workforce has the necessary skills to support the maintenance, development and expansion of a first-class, cost-effective twenty-first century railway.

Promoting UK Leadership in Rail Innovation

12.24 The UK remains at the forefront of research, design and innovation in the rail sector. It has an ambitious agenda to improve customer satisfaction and capacity, while driving down costs and carbon emissions.

12.25 Government, industry, and the research sector work in partnership through the rail industry Technical Strategy Advisory Group. This work is leading to the development of new approaches, products and services, from adapting to the impacts of climate change to understanding whole system reliability.

---

14 http://www.bis.gov.uk/policies/skills-for-growth
15 http://www.bis.gov.uk/policies/higher-ambitions

New Industry, New Jobs

> **LPA** is a leading designer, manufacturer and supplier of environmentally sustainable LED lamps and other electronic and electro-mechanical systems.
>
> Train operators around the world choose LPA's cost-effective solutions and products for their known ability to enhance reliability and reduce maintenance and life cycle costs. Its LED lamps, for example, last up to 30 times longer than halogen lamps, use one-fifth of the energy and deliver 20 per cent more light. A major train operator is successfully trialling LPA LED lamps following its experience of energy shortages resulting from halogen lamps which are more energy intensive and can require daily maintenance. The system is running maintenance-free and releasing enough spare energy to run a hot drinks vending machine, providing the operator with an opportunity to increase revenue.

12.26 Evidence suggests that more could be done to accelerate the introduction of new technology, products and systems. To help identify and better understand the key barriers to innovation, the Government has commissioned new research and with the industry is considering the case for new testing facilities.

12.27 In addition, the Technology Strategy Board is currently working across the surface transport sector, including rail, maritime, automotive, intelligent transport systems and low carbon transport, to establish a new Knowledge Transfer Network (KTN). The new KTN will support the exchange of knowledge, information and ideas across the transport sector. This will include work with the rail supply chain and associated industry partners to identify where innovative new products and services can be developed.

Supporting UK Exports

12.28 Many countries are now looking at high speed rail as a sustainable way to improve their future transport infrastructure. Huge global investment is underway, from China to Europe, the Middle East and the USA. The UK already has much to offer rail export markets, with its global reputation for quality and excellence. A new high speed line would greatly enhance the UK's capability and provide a show case for British expertise.

12.29 To support the UK rail sector overseas, UK Trade and Investment (UKTI), working in partnership with the rail industry, has an active programme of export support. This includes inward and outward trade missions, and UKTI will host a major international rail seminar to promote UK expertise in May 2010.

Arup and Terry Farrell & Partners: Beijing South Railway Station

The new Beijing South railway station is an architectural icon for China's capital city. It is a fully integrated multi-modal transport hub that serves as a "Gateway" to the capital and a vital link in China's new high speed inter-city network.

The state-of-the-art station is one of the largest contemporary railway stations in the world, designed for a passenger throughput of 286,500 passengers a day, 105 million passengers annually by 2030. It provides 28 high speed, urban, inter-city and mass transit platforms as well as large bus interchange and car parking areas.

A team of the UK's Terry Farrell & Partners (a firm of internationally recognised architects and urban designers) and Arup (a UK-based, independent firm of designers, planners, engineers, consultants and technical specialists), together with Chinese design partners, led and developed the scheme.

Terry Farrell & Partners developed the master plan and architectural design for the station and the surrounding area, integrating the rail infrastructure with Beijing's urban fabric. Arup developed the initial structural roof scheme with their Chinese design partners, and were responsible for approval of the schematic, preliminary design and detailed design of the large-scale multi-span, steel cable beam supported roof. Arup also managed the wind tunnel testing for the building's unique form and provided advanced engineering techniques for assessing air quality and indoor airflow, developing a combined cooling/heating power system, and performing annual energy consumption analysis.

Conclusion

This Command Paper responds to HS2 Ltd's recommended route for a high speed line from London to the West Midlands, as well as its assessment of a number of options for a wider initial core high speed network linking the major cities of the Midlands and the North, and stretching to Scotland. It has also examined the case for high speed rail as a potential core element of the UK's twenty-first century inter-urban transport infrastructure.

The Government has reviewed the detailed proposals put forward by HS2 Ltd for a high speed line from London to the West Midlands, and considers, subject to further work on mitigating specific local and environmental impacts, that HS2 Ltd's recommended route could form a viable foundation for such a network.

The Government has also considered HS2 Ltd's advice on the potential development of a high speed link beyond the West Midlands. The Government's view, subject to consultation, is that there is a case for a core high speed rail network linking London to Birmingham, Manchester, the East Midlands, Sheffield and Leeds, with connections to existing main line routes to extend direct high speed services to other cities including Liverpool, Newcastle, Glasgow and Edinburgh.

The Government has therefore asked HS2 Ltd to commence similar detailed planning work on potential route options for high speed lines from Birmingham on to Manchester and Leeds.

On the basis of HS2 Ltd's recommendations and advice, the Government's view is that a high speed rail network offers a balance of benefits unmatched by any other option and should be at the heart of the long-term development of inter-city travel in Britain.

A project of the scope of a new high speed line has implications for many individuals, families, communities and businesses. No firm decision can be made by the Government either on its preferred route for any specific line, or on its proposed strategy for high speed rail, until formal public consultation has taken place, in which all those affected by or interested in its proposals have the opportunity to participate.

The Government will begin such a formal public consultation in the autumn in respect of its preferred route option for a London to Birmingham line and on its overall strategy for high speed rail. This will provide all those interested in or affected by its proposals with the opportunity to express their views. Subject to the results of that consultation, the Government plans in due course to consult in the same way on detailed options for the Manchester and Leeds legs of a core network.

Following completion of these consultations, as well as further development work and financial and environmental assessment, if the Government's conclusion is that a British high speed network should be delivered, and that the routes proposed are viable, it will commission HS2 Ltd to begin the work needed to prepare for seeking the necessary powers via a Hybrid Bill.

This process would be consistent with opening the first leg of High Speed Two in 2026.